MSGR. CASIMIR F. DURAND

THE OLD CATHOLIC CHURCH AND OTHER WRITINGS

EDITED, COLLECTED,

AND INTRODUCED

BY

SERGE A. THERIAULT

To the glory of God, in memory of the Rev. Dr. Jean N. Bodot (1874-1939), appreciated collaborator of Bishop Durand.

Dedicated to my wife Diane, our daughter Melanie, our two sons John and Justin, and our granddaughter Veronica.

Apocryphile press
1700 Shattuck Ave #81
Berkeley, CA 94709

www.apocryphile.org

© 2010

ISBN: 978-1-937002-16-9

Copies of this book are available from www.amazon.com or by writing:

The Christian Catholic Church in the Capital Area
Saint Bernard and Saint Gregory
30 Briermoor Crescent
Ottawa (ON), Canada K1T 3G7

TABLE OF CONTENTS

Msgr. Casimir F. Durand succeeded Msgr. Rene Vilatte (1854-1929) as 2nd Ordinary of the Christian Catholic Church (C.C.C.)[1] and 4th President of the American Catholic Church (A.C.C.), a council of churches organized under the aegis of the C.C.C.[2]

---

[1] The Christian Catholic Church (C.C.C.) comes from a reform originating in the French Canadian parish of St. Anne (Kankakee), Illinois, U.S.A. in the middle of the 19th century. Michel Drolet, Moise Langelier, Joseph Martin, Louis Mercier, Abraham Pelletier, Anselme Robillard and the priest Charles Chiniquy (1809-1899) directed the first society, registered at the Court of Kankakee September 13, 1859. In 1885, parishes were founded among the French-speaking colonists of Wisconsin, by the Reverend Rene Vilatte sent from St. Anne, IL, by Father Chiniquy. The ministry was extended to the Canadian provinces of Ontario and Quebec. Its centre is in Ottawa-Gatineau. The work was organized into an Incorporated Synod under the Reverend Vilatte, elected as bishop. He was consecrated in 1892, by an Independent Catholic Church in Sri Lanka, attached to the Syriac Patriarchate of Antioch. The C.C.C. is a member of the International Council of Community Churches. It is also known as the *Christian Catholic Rite of Community Churches*. More details on the C.C.C. can be found in my book Msgr. Rene Vilatte, Community Organizer of Religion, Apocryphile Press, Berkeley, 2006.

[2] The A.C.C. "brings together in visible bonds of unity other bodies while each remains independent and carries on its work in its own sphere". The Year Book of the Churches 1924, Federal Council of the Churches of Christ in America, New York, p. 13). It was organized on August 20, 1894, during a synod assembled in Cleveland, Ohio. Polish speaking churches first joined, then other groups starting with Italian Americans (1908) and a protocol was signed on January 1, 1910, by Msgr. Vilatte and the bishops he had consecrated for them (document in the Appendix, p. 93). The A.C.C. was incorporated on July 13, 1915. One of the trustees was Bishop Frederick E.J. Lloyd. He became President (Primate) of the A.C.C. during a synod held in Chicago on April 10, 1920. Msgr. Vilatte reminded him in a letter dated March 17, 1920 (document, page 31) that the A.C.C. was formed under the aegis of the C.C.C., (also called Old Roman Catholic Church in those days), based on its Apostolic Succession and its doctrinal statement (published in 1890 under the name *Sketch of the Beliefs*). The three first Presidents were: Bishop Vilatte (1894-1920), Bishop Lloyd (1920-1932) and Bishop Daniel Hinton (1932-1940).

Formerly a Canon Regular (of St. Augustine) of the Immaculate Conception in France, he came to work as a missionnary in Canada at the end of the 19th century. He joined the church in Chicago where he was studying Naturopathic Medicine and was ordained priest there. He exercised his ministry in Chicago (1916-1917), in Windsor, Ontario (1918-1922) and in Minneapolis, Minnesota (1923-1957), while practicing as a Naturopathic Doctor.

His work is made of the essay *The Old Catholic Church*, which is reproduced in Part I, and of other writings which will be found in Part II, including *The Call of the American Catholic Church*, a presentation he made in Chicago in 1917.

Historical texts of interest were found in Bishop Durand's papers. I have reproduced them in the Appendix, including *The Smaller Catechism* compiled and published in 1915.[3]

Acknowledgement

This book would not have been possible without the collaboration of Bishop Durand's twin sons Paul and Rene of Minnesota (now deceased), and of his granddaughter Bonnie Norman of California, to whom I express my deepest gratitude.

---

[3]   By Bishop Lloyd, with the Imprimatur of Bishop Vilatte.

BIOGRAPHICAL CHRONOLOGY
OF THE RT REV. DR. DURAND

Dr. Durand was born in Glandage, a small village in the Rhône-Alpes region of France, on September 19, 1879 the second son of Jean-Antoine Durand and Julie Chancel. He grew up and received his early education in his village.

1892-1899

On August 15, 1892 he entered the juniorate of the Canons Regular (of St. Augustine) of the Immaculate Conception (C.R.I.C.)[4] at Saint-Antoine l'Abbaye in Isère. He took the religious habit on March 7, 1893; made his vows on June 11, 1898 and left for Canada to do his scholasticate at Notre Dame de Lourdes in Manitoba, under Dom Paul Benoît, Ph.D., Th.D.[5] He helped at the parish church and also at Saint Alphonse nearby.

---

[4] The C.R.I.C. are a Roman Catholic congregation which follows the Augustinian Rule, and part of the Order of the Canons Regular of St. Augustine. This order was founded at Saint-Claude (Jura) and later at Saint-Antoine l'Abbaye (Isère), France. The first members took their vows in 1866. The Congregation undertook the restoration of the full canonical life with its primitive observances, the recitation of the Divine Office day and night, perpetual abstinence and the fasts of earlier times. Their object being to unite the practices of ordinary religious life with clerical functions, principally in the administration of pastoral duties in parishes and the education of young clerics. http://en.wikipedia.org/wiki/Canons_Regular_of_the_Immaculate_Conception

[5] Paul Benoît (1850-1915), from Eastern France, was C.R.I.C. Abbot's delegate for the Order's houses in North America. He set up the colony of Notre Dame de Lourdes near Pembina Mountain in Manitoba.

1900-1906

On September 11, 1900, he left the C.R.I.C. and went to work as a missionary to the Cree,[6] according to his sons. This could explain why he was in Saint Paul, Minnesota, in 1903. It was a place of expertise in Native North American ministry. Due to a lack of medical care available, he made use, in his ministry, of the knowledge in herbal medicine he had obtained from the old monks of the Abbey of St. Anthony.[7] This experience oriented him towards Naturopathy[8] inspired by Austrian priest Sebastian Kneipp.[9]

1907-1913

Returning from France (Saint Antoine l'Abbaye) through Quebec City on the ship Virginian, on September 20, 1907 he declared to

---

[6]   Cree, also called Chippewa, Assiniboin, Dakota, are one of the two greatest divisions of the Algonquian linguistic family. When they first came to the knowledge of Europeans they extended from James Bay to Saskatchewan.
http://www.canadiangenealogy.net/indians/cree_indians.htm

[7]   See his text *Taking care of the body as well as the soul with the healing methods learnt from the old Monks of St. Anthony* on page 63.

[8]   In the USA, the term naturopathy was coined before 1900 by Scheel, and used by Benedict Lust. Lust had been schooled in hydrotherapy and other natural health practices in Germany by Father Sebastian Kneipp, who sent Lust to the United States to bring them Kneipp's methods. In 1905, Lust founded the American School of Naturopathy in New York, the first naturopathic college in the United States.

[9]   Father Kneipp (1821-1897) created a life philosophy that sees humans going about their daily habits and routines in their natural habitat as an inseparable entity. http://kneippus.com/sebastian-kneipp.html

be botanist (herbalist) and to reside in Minneapolis. He is listed as Physician in the 1909 City Directory. His office was at 823 Fifth Ave South.

In 1912, he studied Homeopathic Medicine at the University of Michigan and during summer, he married Anna de Mancip in La Beaume (Isère), France. He is listed among the graduates of Michigan University Homeopathic Medical School in the Annual Announcement of 1913.

1914-1917

A doctoral student at the Lindlahr College of Natural Therapeutics in Chicago,[10] he made contact with Bishop Vilatte and the cathedral parish at 4427 N. Mulligan Avenue. He wrote to the bishop that he admired him and liked to read his writings.[11] From this period date his poem *Free, Catholic and Gallican* and his essay *National Churches dominated by the Roman Curia and being suppressed.*[12]

---

[10]   Henry Lindlahr (1862–1924) was the founder of *Scientific Naturopathy* in the United States. He took his training in Nature Cure in Europe, under Father Kneipp, before opening his practice in Chicago in 1902. Eventually the practice expanded to include Lindlahr College to train physicians and nurses in his methods of treatment. See the text *Dr. Lindlahr Nature Cure Approach* in the Appendix, p. 87.

[11]   More specifically *What was Catholic once must be forever* and *We maintain the faith once for all given to the saints*. The letter can be found in Chapter 2, page 67, and the texts in the Appendix, p. 97-101.

[12]   Texts in Chapter 2, p. 71-78.

He was naturalized as U.S. citizen on September 11, 1915 and on December 29 he attended the consecration of Bishop Frederick E.J. Lloyd in Chicago.[13] He was ordained at that time by Bishop Vilatte, for ministry at St. David's Chapel, 536 E. 36th Street.[14] He is mentioned as priest-in-charge in the Chicago Tribune, from Feb. 5, 1916 to Sept. 1, 1917. He used in his ministry the *Catechism* compiled and published in 1915 by Bishop Lloyd.[15]

On October 24, 1917, his twin sons Paul and René[16] were born. The attending physician was Dr. Edwin B. Beckwith, a friend who was also parish priest of the Liberal Catholic Church in Chicago. The family was living at 505 E. 30th Street. The same year, he was called up and resided on the military base in Wayne, Michigan. Mrs. Durand and the children went to live with Bishop Vilatte on North Mulligan Ave. Rene bears his name and Paul, that of Bishop Miraglia-Gullotti, Auxiliary for the Italian Americans. He had been forced into retirement because of ill health and was staying at the bishopric with Bishop Vilatte. He died from myocarditis on July 25, 1918.

---

[13]   See the Invitation card on page 26.

[14]   Bishop Vilatte is alluding to Fr. Durand ordained by him in a letter to Bishop Lloyd. See page 34.

[15]   Dr. Durand's copy is reproduced in the Appendix, p. 103-118.

[16]   See the statement I signed with them about their father's papers and their biographical sketch, in the Appendix, p. 133-134.

1918-1922

He was missionary priest and Naturopathic Doctor in Windsor (Ontario), Canada. His centre was at 245 Ouellette Avenue. He also served as Principal of the Theological Department of the A.C.C.[17]

On September 28, 1921 he witnessed the consecration, by Msgr. Vilatte, of Dr. George A. McGuire[18] for the African Orthodox Church (A.O.C.), and signed the consecration certificate.[19] The following year, he founded the Border Cities Hospital in Windsor (ON), on the model of the Lindlahr Sanitarium.[20]

1923-1925

He was parish priest in Minneapolis. « *Paul remembers his dad's*

---

[17]   Listed as such in the *Year Book of the Churches*, National Council of the Churches of Christ in the U.S.A., New York, 1919, p. 78.

[18]   George A. McGuire (1866-1934) was the founder and first bishop of the A.O.C. He entered the Jefferson Medical College of Philadelphia, graduating in 1910. He served as both minister and physician in the U.S.A. and the West Indies. During his travels, he befriended Marcus Garvey, the widely known defender of the rights of the African Americans, and became convinced of the singular importance of establishing the A.O.C.

[19]   Document on page 35. It is interesting to note that both Father Durand and Father Ernest Robertson, the other witness and co-signator of the consecration certificate, were to succeed their Ordinary, one in 1926, the other in 1934.

[20]   *New Incorporations*, The Monetary Times, Toronto, August 11, 1922, p. 10. More on the Lindlahr Sanitarium in the Appendix, p. 90.

church at 1705 Nicollet Avenue, wrote his niece Bonnie, *½ block north of Franklin Avenue. He and René would carry a banner together down the church aisle at the beginning of the service. Mom*, he said, *made the vestments for both dad and the other priests.*"[21]

In June 1923, he became Vicar General of the C.C.C. at the time of Bishop Vilatte's departure for France, to establish an Extension of the A.C.C. The goal was *to restore the Orthodox Catholic faith in France.*[22] It was located at 48 Vauban Ave in Gargan,[23] a commune in the northeastern suburbs of Paris (9.7 miles from the center of Paris). On October 10, he issued from there a bull giving authority for the consecration of Father Ernest Robertson, elected Auxiliary to Bishop McGuire.[24] He also led from there the Order of the Crown of Thorns (O.C.T.),[25] using O.C.T. letterhead when writing to persons who were members of the Order. Both works he did till he retired to the Pont Colbert Cistercian Abbey in Versailles in 1925.

---

[21]   Bonnie (Durand) Norman in an eMail dated Sept. 24, 2005.

[22]   Letter of Msgr. Vilatte to Bishop Jean Bricaud of Lyon, 20 July 1924.

[23]   See the *carte de visite* reproduced on page 36.

[24]   The bull was read during the consecration in the Cathedral Chapel of the Good Shepherd in New York, on Sunday November 18, 1923.

[25]   The O.C.T. is a chivalrous and religious order organized in America on June 1, 1891. The order was inspired from a similar order founded in 1239, to protect the Crown of Thorns of our Lord Jesus Christ inherited from the Holy Land by St. Louis, King of France.

At 47, he became the 2nd Ordinary of the C.C.C. *"Dr. C.F. Durand will be consecrated a bishop,* can we read in Minneapolis papers (15 Sept.)*, at the (Polish National) Church of the Sacred Heart of Jesus, 23rd Ave and 5th S. N.E. tomorrow at 10:30 A.M. Dr. A. Fryxell of Seattle, Bishop of the Swedish Church in America will perform the ceremony which will be open to the public."*

On September 19, he sat on the *Mid-West Mission Board* as Vice-President. The Board was to be called together by the President, Bishop Fryxell, or in his absence, by the Vice-President, as often as needed. Its object was to plan for mission work and to collect money to carry on church work. Bishop Durand had the right to use his own discretion to decide when the money should be spent and where help was most needed for extending the work. Other Board members were: the Rev. Ernst V. Eckström, Secretary, and Prof. Dr. G.A. Montelius, Treasurer. [26]

Dr. Durand's papers indicate that the Rev. Kazimierz Krysinski, pastor of Sacred Heart Church (Minneapolis), was invested *Chevalier Commandeur* of the O.C.T.[27] The Grand Masters of the

---

[26]   The Rev. Eckström was ordained by Bishop Fryxell in June 1925 for the Minneapolis Swedish Mission. Dr. Montelius was a dentist teaching at the university. Information found in Dr. Durand's papers (news clipping).

[27]   See *Twin Cities* newspaper clipping (Minneapolis/Saint Paul), p. 38.

Order have been the Ordinaries of the C.C.C., starting with Bishop Vilatte, to whom succeeded Dr. Durand.

1928-1929

In the April issue of the A.C.C. newsletter *The Antiochean*, Dr. Durand is indicated as bishop of the French-speaking constituency (C.C.C.), with Dr. J. Nicholas Bodot as collaborator.[28] His ministry was in Syracuse, N.Y.

In May, Henri Perdriau[29] of Rhode Island gave him his support and invited the Franco-Americans to join the church. He published under Bishop Durand's Imprimatur, and with his collaboration, the brochure called *Fiat Lux – Le bon sens et la logique* (Common Sense and Logic).[30] It was written after Rome had excommunicated the leaders of a movement that was opposing Roman Catholic Bishop W. Hickey of Providence, under

---

[28]   Text in the Appendix, p. 121. Dr. Bodot was a Chiropractor. He joined the church under the influence of his wife's family (Lavaute from St. Ursula Falls, Quebec) who were members. Patricia D. DiFlorio, <u>John Nicholas and Marianne Muehler Bodot Family</u>, Syracuse NY, 2007, p. 7. He was ordained priest by Bishop Vilatte sometime in 1910.

[29]   Formerly a Trappist monk, H. Perdriau (1877-1950) was a renown stained glass artist turned journalist. His works can be found on large buildings such as: the National Assembly of Quebec (the library) and St. Joseph Oratory in Montreal (the crypt). In 1923 he had settled in Rhode Island, where his former apprentice Guido Nincheri was decorating Franco-American churches, including St. Anne of Woonsocket.

[30]   Summary of the brochure in the Appendix, p. 123-127.

the auspices of the newspaper *La Sentinelle* of Woonsocket, where Perdriau was journalist. Bishop Hickey was forcing the French speaking parishes of his diocese to fund English schools only, through compulsory taxes.

Bishop Durand wrote his essay *The Old Catholic Church* while he was in Woonsocket (21-28 August) to establish a Franco-American parish. He celebrated the inaugural Mass on Sunday, August 26, with 65 people in attendance.[31]

The Woonsocket parish was short-lived. Eventually, the excommunicated protesters were readmitted to communion to the Roman Catholic Church. It was, needless to say, a result inversely proportional to the investment and Bishop Durand came out *écorché* of this episode of his episcopate. He was denounced by Henri Bourassa, the Director of the Montreal newspaper *Le Devoir*, in a series of articles written between 15-18 January 1929. The third article, published on January 17, and titled *Schisme gallican "orthodoxe"* ("Orthodox" Gallican Schism) was particularly sarcastic. [32]

---

[31] Robert Rumilly, Histoire des Franco-Américains, Union Saint-Jean-Baptiste d'Amérique, 1958, p. 445.

[32] Henri Bourassa, (1868-1952), politician, journalist and spokesman for Canadian nationalism. He embraced ultramontanism, a movement that stresses papal authority rather than nationalism in the church. MacMillan, Michael C., "The Character of Henri Bourassa's Political Philosophy", *American Review of Canadian Studies* 1982b 12(1): 10-29.

In the month of July, he was saddened by the passing of Bishop Vilatte in Versailles, France[33] and on September 29-30, he attended the A.C.C. Synod convened in Chicago by Bishop Lloyd.[34] Other bishops present were: Axel Fryxell of Seattle, Daniel Hinton, Coadjutor, Gregory Lines of Los Angeles, Francis Kanski of Chicago, Ernest Peterson of Miami[35] and Churchill Sibley, consecrated for Great Britain during synod.

1930

In January, he took notice of the founding of the *Société des Amis de Mgr Vilatte* by Mr. A. Jouanny of Paris. The goals were to maintain the grave of the good bishop and defend his memory. The work of the *Société* is continued in Canada by the C.C.C., including the maintenance of Bishop Vilatte's tombstone in Gonards Cemetery.

In the following month, he greeted Msgr. Francis I. Boryszewski whom Msgr. Lloyd had consecrated (2 Feb.) for the A.C.C. Polish constituency, with Mariavite Old Catholic Bishop Roman J.

---

[33] He died on July 1 and was buried in Gonards Cemetery (Versailles) on July 3.

[34] *The American Catholic Church Starts Its Session on Sunday*, Chicago Tribune, September 27, 1929.

[35] They were consecrated by Bishop Lloyd (Hinton on March 27, 1927, Lines on July 1, 1923, Peterson on June 5, 1927), except Kanski who was consecrated by Bishop Vilatte on January 22, 1923.

Prochniewski [36] of Plock, Poland. This consecration marked a change in the policy of the church regarding Roman Catholic Orders.[37] In 1945, Msgr. Prochniewski would consecrate for Hungary +Tomasz Czernohorsky-Fehervary (1917-1984) [38] who ordained priest and mitred my predecessor +O'Neill Côté (1939-1986). He was Episcopal Visitor of the Christian Catholics in Quebec till 1978, when the ministry of the C.C.C. was incorporated into the Independent Catholic Church of Canada.[39]

On July 1, 1930, he (Bishop Durand) ordered that this date be a festival of thanks for the labors of Bishop Vilatte who entered on

---

36   The Mariavite Old Catholic Church, from Latin words: *Mariae vitam* – following/imitating the life of Mary, developed out of a community of sisters founded by Feliksa Kozłowska in Plock in 1887 and a community of secular priests organized in 1906 in Warsaw at her instigation by Jan Michal Kowalski. Both groups aimed at religious, moral and social renewal of clergy and people. Bishop Prochniewski was consecrated on October 5, 1909 by the Archbishop of Utrecht, Gerard Gul, and Bishop J.M. Kowalski.

37   The policy was that there is no true Apostolic Succession in the Church of Rome. See the statement *Why the A.C.C. cannot accept Roman Catholic Orders* (1917) by Bishop Miraglia-Gullotti and his poem *Fredericus Lloyd Americae Episcopus* (1915) on the unique See of St. Peter at Antioch (Unica Petri Sede) in the Appendix, p. 119-120. The two documents were found in the papers of Bishop Durand.

38   Exiled to Montreal for political reasons in 1965, Bishop Fehervary organized a parish that was built around a group of immigrants of Austro-Hungarian heritage who, like him, came to Canada, following the failure of the Hungarian revolt.

39   At a synod held in Niagara Falls (Ont.) on July 1-2, 1978, Msgr. Côté was elected and consecrated as Bishop of Quebec. The Primate was +Peter W. Goodrich: http://www.independentanglicanchurch.ca/.

that day in 1929 into the Church Triumphant. The initiative for that festival came from the A.O.C. Their synod had passed a resolution to that effect (The Negro Churchman, Vol. 8, No. 6, June-July 1930).

1932-1942

He welcomed Bishop Daniel Hinton who succeeded Msgr. Lloyd as President of the A.C.C. on February 12, 1932.[40] He kept in his papers an Official Statement on the A.C.C. that Bishop Hinton made in 1936.[41] His office, in those years, was located at 2101 Portland Ave South, Minneapolis.

Bishop Hinton having resigned, Father W. Sullivan,[42] the Chancellor of A.C.C., asked him to take the presidency. He accepted the charge as evidenced by the letter he addressed to him on July 15, 1940 [43] and which is kept in our church holding at the National Archives of Quebec.

---

[40]   Bishop Lloyd was forced to retire because of ill health. He died on September 11, 1933 in Chicago.

[41]   The Statement was published in the A.C.C. newsletter (then called The Crusader), in November 1936. Dr. Durand's copy is reproduced in the Appendix, p. 129.

[42]   The Rev. Sullivan of 4054 Oakwood Ave, Chicago, was a priest of the A.C.C. who was professor of languages in the Endich Theological Seminary organized for the training of A.O.C. clergy.

[43]   The letter can be found on pages 83-84.

Eventually, the A.C.C. ceased to exist as the council of churches formed under the aegis of the C.C.C. Colonel William Siple of the German American constituency [44] was appointed as lay administrator of the corporation. The appointment was made in concertation with Bishop Kanski of Chicago who had been looking after the North Mulligan Ave church since Bishop Vilatte had left for France. His residence was at 6417 Forest Preserve Drive which became the principal address of the A.C.C.[45] Colonel Siple took office on April 26, 1943 and when he died in 1964, he had liquidated the assets of the corporation.[46] The original jurisdiction (C.C.C.), registered in Illinois in 1859 and incorporated in Wisconsin in 1890, continues in Canada, where it was granted Letters Patent under the Law on Religious Corporations of Quebec.

Dr. Durand died from a heart attack on January 6, 1957 in Prior Lake (Scott County), Minnesota, where he had been living since 1932. His wife Anna joined him 21 years later, on May 25, 1978.

---

[44] Led by the Rev. William Oscar Homburger (abbreviated Homer) who had been Chancellor of the A.C.C. under Bishops Lloyd and Hinton. He was associated with Msgr. Fryxell, who consecrated him bishop on March 14, 1930.

[45] See the document *Amendment to the Articles of Incorporation of the A.C.C.* re: principal address of the corporation in the Appendix, p. 130.

[46] Information provided by Paul Durand, in a telephone conversation I had with him in April 1997.

Glandage (Drôme), France

Saint Antoine l'Abbaye (Isère), France

Bro. Casimir, C.R.I.C., 1898

Church & Priory, Notre Dame de Lourdes, MB, 1900

You are invited to be present at the Consecration of the Rev. Frederic E. J. Lloyd, D. D., as Suffragan-Bishop (with the title of Bishop of Illinois), to the Most Rev. Archbishop Vilatte, Primate and Metropolitan, which will take place Wednesday, December 29th, in St. David's Chapel, 536 East 36th Street, Chicago, at 10:30 A. M., the Archbishop being Consecrator. Please reply to 3657 Grand Boulevard.

Invitation to Bishop Lloyd's consecration

St. David's Mission

American Catholic Church
536 East 36th Street
CHICAGO
Rt. Rev. Frederic E. J. Lloyd, D.D.

Services
(In English)

Sunday—Mass at 8 and 10:30 a. m.
Sunday School—3:00 p. m.
Vespers and Sermon—7:30 p. m.

Wednesday, Friday and
Saints' Days—

Mass at 8:00 a. m.

The poor, the sorrowful, the bereaved, the friendless, the helpless, hopeless and the perplexed will always find a friend at the Mission House.

Bishop Lloyd may be seen daily except Monday from 9:00 o'clock to noon, or at other times by appointment.

The American Catholic Church does not take its orders or complexion from Rome, Moscow, Canterbury or other foreign source. It is the only truly national Catholic Church for the United States. Other Churches in the United States are not American, nor do they claim to be. The Apostolic Succession of the American Catholic Church is derived from the apostolic see of Antioch of which St. Peter was the founder. Its faith is that of the undivided Holy Catholic Church before 1054. It is not Roman Catholic, neither is it Protestant—it is loyally and enthusiastically American, Catholic, and Apostolic.

Bishop Vilatte and Bishop Lloyd.
With them on the picture, priests F. Kanski and T. Peshkoff

Bishop Paul Miraglia-Gullotti [47]

The Rev. Edwin B. Beckwith, A.B., M.D.

---

[47]   Consecrated by Bishop Vilatte on May 6, 1900, he was co-consecrator of Bishop Lloyd.

Durand Family in Chicago

Michigan Homeopathic School

Lindlahr College

REGISTRATION CARD

SERIAL NUMBER 6869

ORDER NUMBER 4943

1 Casimir Felix Durand
(First name) (Middle name) (Last name)

2 PERMANENT HOME ADDRESS: Detroit – Mich.
(No.) (Street or R. F. D. No.) (City or town) (County) (State)

Age in Years 3 39

Date of Birth 4 Sept 19th 1879
(Month.) (Day.) (Year.)

RACE

White	Negro	Oriental	Indian	
			Citizen	Noncitizen
5 Yes	6 ✓	7 ✓	8 ✓	9 ✓

U. S. CITIZEN

ALIEN

| Native Born | Naturalized | Citizen by Father's Naturalization Before Registrant's Majority | Declarant | Non-declarant |
| 10 No | 11 Yes | 12 No | 13 ✓ | 14 ✓ |

15 If not a citizen of the U. S. of what nation are you a citizen or subject? USA

| PRESENT OCCUPATION | EMPLOYER'S NAME |
| 16 Missionary Priest | 17 ✓ |

18 PLACE OF EMPLOYMENT OR BUSINESS: Royal Bank Bldg – Windsor – Ont.
(No.) (Street or R. F. D. No.) (City or town) (County) (State)

NEAREST RELATIVE
19 Name Anna S. Durand – (Wife)
20 Address 4427 N. Mulligan Ave – Chicago – Ills.
(No.) (Street or R. F. D. No.) (City or town) (County) (State)

I AFFIRM THAT I HAVE VERIFIED ABOVE ANSWERS AND THAT THEY ARE TRUE

P. M. G. O.
Form No. 1 (Red) Casimir F. Durand
(Registrant's signature or mark)

Dr. Lindlahr

Fr. Kneipp

Missionary priest in Windsor ON

Letter of Msgr. Vilatte to Bishop Lloyd, 1920.03.17:
A.C.C. formed under the C.C.C. (Old R. Catholic Church)
based on its Apostolic Succession and Profession of Faith

EX ORIENTE LUX!

The American ▮▮▮ Catholic Church

INCORPORATED AS

THE OLD ROMAN CATHOLIC CHURCH OF AMERICA

Apostolic Succession from the See of St. Peter Through the
Favor of His Holiness Ignatius Peter III.-Patriarch of Antioch

MOST REV. ARCHBISHOP J. R VILATTE

4427 N MULLIGAN AVENUE
JEFFERSON STATION

Saint Patrick Day.

Chicago, Ill. March 17ᵗʰ 1920

To the Rt Rev. F. J. Lloyd, D.D.

Bishop of Illinois

Chicago Illinois.

My dear Bishop Lloyd:-

your two outspoken and
heart-to-heart letters found
me in loving sympathy with
you — I will briefly reply to
your point by point.

(1) The Synod of the American
Catholic Church you have called
for April 10ᵗʰ next has my
full approbation and blessing.

(2) I hereby, ex tota corde,
make you leader with full
power over The American Catholic Church; this ipso facto
supersedes the position you
have hitherto to held as

31

(2) my suffragan and Bishops of Illinois.

(3) If your clergy at the coming Synod, make you their Arch-bishop - Elect, be assured this Election will receive my hearty approval and blessing, and I shall receive you as Arch-bishop of the American Catholic Church.

(4) Personally I desire no change to Exarch. I was consecrated Archbishop, Metropolitan, and Primate for the Old (Roman) Catholic Church of America, and such I shall live and die. By "watching over you" and others deriving Orders from me, I mean simply the deter-mination to hold you all to the Profession of Faith, you swore to as the condition sine qua non

(3) on which I ordained or consecrated you.

(5) In regard to the Constitution and Canons of your branch of the Church you will no doubt take care that nothing may be adopted contrary to dogmas of the Seven Ecumenic Councils, and that the disciplinary rules be not contrary to universal Catholic Teaching and customs,

(6) Let me say from my heart to you, that the American Catholic Church with one Archbishop and ten (?) priests of years quite top-heavy enough. If in the course of a year your followers should greatly augment doubtless the fitting man for a new bishop or bishops would appear.

(4) Believe me to remain dear Brother,
Affectionately yours.

+ J. R. Vilatte Catholic
Archbishop, Metropolitan and Primate
Supreme Presiding Prelate

P.S. If Fathers Sneed and Durand
or others
desire to be under your jurisdiction, I am not opposed.
As for Father Nybladh, you
ordained him and he swore
obedience to you.

Bishop Vilatte alluding to Fr. Durand ordained by him.

In the Name of the Father, and of the Son,
and of the Holy Spirit, Amen!

JOSEPH RENE VILATTE, by Divine Providence and the favor of the
Patriarchal See of Saint Peter at Antioch, Archbishop & Metropolitan,
Exarch of the American Catholic Church to all who may see these
health, peace and benediction in Christ Jesus Our Lord!
Know ye all men by these present letters that on Wednes- day
the twenty-eighth of the month of September of the One
Thousand Nine Hundred and twenty-first in the year
of Our Lord in the Church of Our Lady of Good Death, 4429 North
Mulligan Avenue, Norwood Park, County of Cook, Illinois, at the request
of and for the African Orthodox Church, and with the assistance of
Our Brother the Right Reverend Carl A. Nybladh, Bishop,
and in the presence of Christians of Our Jurisdiction and others, by
virtue of the powers conferred upon Us in the One Holy Catholic
and Apostolic Church and in accordance with the Constitution of
the American Catholic Church, We have imposed Our Hands upon,
and consecrated to the Sacred Order of the Episcopate: the Priest
GEORGE ALEXANDER McGUIRE, Bishop of the AFRICAN ORTHODOX CHURCH;

In testimony whereof We hereunto affix Our Hand and Seal
on this twenty-eighth day of the month of September of the
One Thousand Nine Hundred and twenty-first
year of Our Lord.

I, the Chancellor of the Church, do hereby certify
that these present letters are recorded in the Archives of the American
Catholic Church and that they have been properly issued in accordance with
the Constitution of the same (No. 102109288A--)
In virtue whereof I have hereunto set my hand and seal
On this 28th day of September A.D.

Consecration certificate of Bishop McGuire
bearing the signature of Msgr. (then Fr.) Durand, 1921

✝

J.R. VILATTE
ARCHEVÊQUE CATHOLIQUE
EXTENSION AMÉRICAINE CATHOLIQUE
48, Avenue Vauban, 48

GARGAN
par LIVRY (Seine-et-Oise)

FRANCE

BULL ALLOWING CONSECRATION
From the Metropolitan

In the Name of the Father, Son, and Holy Spirit. Amen.

We, Mar Timotheus I, Archbishop Metropolitan and Exarch in the One Holy Catholic Apostolic Church, hereby allow the consecration of Rev. W. E. Robertson, priest ordained by Us, in the year 1921.

We stand before God's Majesty and raising up our hands towards this Venerable Priest pray that the Holy Gost descend upon him, as He did upon the Apostles and were authorized to bind and loose as written by St. Matthew.

We, therefore, by virtue of our authority received from God, authorize His Grace, the Most Rev. George Alexandre McGuire, to consecrate in episcopal dignity the Priest W. E. Robertson elected Auxiliary Bishop under the jurisdiction of His Grace our well-beloved Brother George Alexandre McGuire.

Given, on the tenth October 1923, from Our Chapel Notre-Dame of France.

✝ MAR TIMOTHEUS I,

(Seal)
Archbishop Vilatte.
Metropolitan and Exarch.

36

Bishop McGuire (2nd) at the consecration of Bishop Daniel Alexander for South Africa (3rd), assisted by Bishops Ernest Robertson (1st) and Arthur S. Trotman (4th) on September 11, 1927. I had the pleasure of admitting Bishop Alexander's successor, the late +Daniel Kanyiles as Prelate Commander of the O.C.T. for Africa.

Bishop Fryxell of the
Swedish Church[48]

Bishop Durand's mozetta
made by his wife Anna

J.N. Bodot

REV. KAZIMIERZ KRYSINSKI, pastor of Sacred Heart Polish National Catholic church and former editor of the Polish weekly, "The Awakening," has received from the Abbey of San Luigi, Order of the Crown of Thorns, the title of "Chevalier Commandeur et Doctor Christianissimus." Well known in Polish literary circles, Mr. Krysinski has written articles for several magazines a n d now is completing a book, "Splashes of the Pen." He was born and educated in Warsaw and attended the Dominican University in Rome.

Rev. Krysinski

---

[48]   Axel Zacharias Fryxell (1860-1934) was consecrated on June 24,1924 by Bishop Lloyd as 2nd Ordinary of the A.C.C. Swedish Constituency. Episcopal See: Seattle, Washington. Pro-Cathedral Church of All Saints.

Fiat Lux !

Vidimus Stellam Ejus Ex Oriente.

. . .

En toute sincérité, nous avons cherché la vérité et Dieu
dans sa miséricorde a permis que nous la trouvions.

⚜ ⚜ ⚜

Le Bon Sens
Et La Logique

Par un catholique qui veut le
devenir davantage encore.

⚜ ⚜ ⚜

Lisez, faites lire à vos amis,
méditez, n'ayez pas peur de la
vérité, celle qui délivre, et sur-
tout agissez; soyez vous-même
missionnaire de-la vérité catholique.

Henri Perdriau

Nihil obstat

Imprimatur

† Casimir

episcopus.

Nicollet Avenue, Minneapolis, 1930s

Dr. Durand and his sons, 1941

Dr. Durand with his wife Anna in their garden
in Prior Lake, Minnesota, 1950s.

Archbishop R.J. Prochniewski, Msgr.
Tomasz C. Fehervary and Msgr. Côté.

Msgr. Côté with Canadian Primate P.W. Goodrich (1st)
and Archbishop J.E. Neth of Florida in Niagara Falls ON,
on July 2, 1978.

I

ESSAY
THE OLD CATHOLIC CHURCH

VISION

We favour a modern revival of Catholicity, as it was understood in the first centuries, guided by the spirit of Christ, our only leader. We labor by this spirit, to put an end to the imperfections and vices that have defiled the Church in the course of time. We do not disown the improvements which reason and the gospel declare to be necessary, but rather insist on their fundamental dependance on Christ and His gospel.

MISSION

We have no intention whatever of founding a new religion or of joining one of the sects that dream of a fanciful Christianity in the future; but faithful to the Church founded by Christ and preached by the apostles, as it appears in the books of the New Testament and in the Christian writings of the first eight centuries[49], we want to live by the spirit of our fathers in the faith, and thus unite the Christian past with the Christian present and the Christian future.

---

[49] It was not until the 9th century that pope Nicolas I fell away from the Eastern Church and caused schism. Although we are Westerners, we do not accept the fault of this pope, and we extend the hand to Christians of the East, inviting them to labor with us for the restoration of union between churches of the East and the West.

Protestation

Convinced that the doctrines of papal infaillibility and the universal jurisdiction of the Bishop of Rome over the Church are erroneous, we do not allow that the dogmatization of these errors by the Pope and the majority of the Council is sufficient to transform them into truths, we reject the two dogmas. It is necessary to recall the proofs established by the Church of the falsity of these two dogmas – a falsity clearly shown up by the Scriptures, by universal tradition, by the history of the seven Ecumenical Councils[50], and by several other undoubted facts. None of these proofs has been seriously refuted by Roman Catholic theologians. We therefore rejecting these new false dogmas, remain faithful to the Catholicity of the time before the Vatican Council (1870); and continue to set the "universal, unvarying, and unanimous" testimony of the Church in opposition to Roman innovations.

This attitude and the theological works which have been produced to prove this truth have led to discover a number of

---

[50] The seven councils are: Nicea I, 325 (defined the divinity of Christ), Constantinople I, 381 (defined the divinity of the Holy Spirit), Ephesus, 431 (defined Christ as Incarnate Word of God and Mary as Theotokos), Chalcedon, 451 (defined Christ as Perfect God and Perfect Man in One Person), Constantinople II, 553 (reconfirmed the doctrines of the Trinity and Christ), Constantinople III, 680 (affirmed the true humanity of Jesus by insisting upon the reality of His human will and action) and Nicea II, 787 (affirmed the propriety of icons as genuine expressions of the Christian Faith).

errors made by the Roman theologians and transformed into dogmas in the course of ages, so that the protest against the false dogmas of the 18th July 1870, has logically incorred the protest against all the false dogmas previously promulgated by the papacy. [51] This discovery of the errors of the Roman Papacy from the 9th century to the present day, and in all the individual churches under the jurisdiction of Rome, has given impetus and importance to our movement.

It is a complete history of Roman theology, remade in accordance with authentic sources and contrary to the thousands of Roman falsifications pointed out recently by eminent theologians of all the churches, including even Roman theologians. We may say that these new publications – this veritable resurrection of ancient documents that we believed buried in darkness – have created a new situation and started a thorough reformation of so-called Catholic theology. This is a part of our work, but it is only one of our proposed aims.

Aims

Our chief aims may be reduced to three: theological reform, ecclesiastical reform, and union of the Christian churches.

---

[51] See Wladimir Guettee, **La Papauté hérétique** (Sandoz & Fishbacher ed., Paris, 1874) and Eugene Michaud, **La Papauté antichrétienne** (Sandoz & Fishbacher, 1873).

Theological Reform

This reform was not undertaken arbitrarily; nor was it conducted by each theologian according to his own personal opinions on each of the disputed questions. A strict method governs all their actions, a method which results especially in distinguishing dogma from theology – dogma which is the word of Christ as it is recorded in the gospel, from theology which is the explanation given by the apostles and scholars to secure the acceptance and practice of the precepts of Jesus Christ.

Christ being "*the way, the truth and the life*" is the only Scholar, the only Master; He has declared it Himself to His disciples. It is therefore He alone who as the only Mediator and Saviour, possesses the words of eternal life; it is He alone who is the light of the world and it is He alone who has the right to impose His doctrines, decrees, dogmas on His disciples.

On the other hand, every disciple is entitled, and even duty bound, to try to understand the dogmas of Christ, to see their depth and beauty, and to derive profit from them for the sanctification of his soul. Dogma is the divine truth taught by Christ, theology is the explanation given by humans – an explanation more or less luminous which each one may judge according to the light of his reason, conscience and knowledge: "*Prove all things; hold fast that which is good*". Thessalonicians 5,21

The distinction between dogma and theology is made by application of the Catholic test to every disputed point. The test is the one so well epitomized by Vincent of Lerins: "*What has been believed everywhere, always and by all the Christian Churches is Catholic*". The Catholic faith is the "universal unvarying, and unanimous faith,

because all the Christian churches cannot be making a mistake when they attest, as a fact, that they have always believed or not believed, from their very foundation, in the doctrine which the Apostles Founders of their particular church has taught them or not. It is not a question of settling an important discussion, but of making a simple statement of fact. As to the theological explanations which may be given of the established doctrine, they depend, like all the explanations of this world, on reason, science, history and all the knowledge which humanity has at its disposal.

Thus faith and liberty are reconciled – the faith which depends not on any caprice of any school, but solely on the historical and objective testimony of the churches; and liberty of criticism or of reason, which belongs to the religious truth transmitted to all the churches, to the best of the religious interests of each church. Thus the faith is a depository – a depository of all the precepts confided by Jesus Christ to His disciples, a depository which does not belong exclusively to one person, but to everybody to the preservation of which all faithful churches carefully attend, so that none of it may be suppressed and also that no foreign doctrine may be sureptitiously introduced into it (depositum custodi).[52] And theology as a science like all other sciences, belongs to reason, to history, to criticism, and obeys fixed rules.

It is therefore neither a bishop, nor a priest, nor a scholar who is entrusted with the preservation of dogma, but all bishops, all priests, all scholars – in a word all the faithful, members of the Church. Christ being the only Master of His Church, there is no other rule than Him that is sufficient to guard his doctrine and

---

[52] "O Timothy, keep that which is committed to thy trust, [Vulg.: depositum custodi] avoiding the profane novelties of words and oppositions of knowledge falsely so called." (1 Tim. 6:20);

precepts. The Church was not instituted to found a religion other than that of Christ, but merely to preserve it and spread it throughout the world: "*Go ye therefore and teach all nations*", Matthew 28,19.

Its mission is not to add to the dogma of Christ, but only to preach them in order to sanctify the world by them (*teaching them to observe all things whatsoever I have commanded*, Matthew 28, 20). The Church is therefore a guardian of the teachings and precepts of Jesus Christ. Its title "the teaching church" means not that it has the right to teach any doctrines that it pleases, but that it is its duty to preach openly what Christ taught His disciples.

Real theological reform should consist in communicating to all the teachings of Jesus Christ as they are collected in the Scriptures and recorded in the universal tradition of the Church – a tradition which also belongs to all the members of the Church. It is the duty of pastors and scholars to explain them and it is the duty of each member to study the explanations which appear wisest and most useful; the good sense and the Christian spirit that prevails in the Church are sufficient to ensure the final triumph of truth over error: "*Where two or three are gathered together in my name, there am I in the midst of them*", Matthew 18,20.

Since the Church is not a chair to which might be addressed all the questions that arise in the minds of the inquisitive and the imaginative, it is not obliged to solve them or to prevent humans from discussing among themselves matters which neither God nor Christ has tought sufficient for the edification and sanctification of humanity. The fruitfulness of the faith does not consist in discovering new dogma (Jude 3) or in transforming the Church into a revealer, charged with completing the revelation made by Christ. The faith which is fruitful increases and grows by closeness of its adherents to the Word of Christ; not by the proclamation of unknown dogmas. It is Christ alone who is the religious light and the religious life of the world; the Church must only be His humble servant.

Ecclesiastical Reform

This reform should consist in reminding the Church what Christ wished it to be. Christ established a hierarchy for the service of the faithful. That hierarchy therefore, ought to serve and not to rule. Its office is a ministry, not an authority. There is no IMPERIUM[53] in the Church of Christ and the obedience of the disciples must be reasonable, and not servile. If any member wanted to be first, he had to be the first to serve his brothers and sisters, and not to give them orders – to feed the flock i.e. to lead it into good pastures and not to enslave it by false dogmas or exploit it by superstitions.

The main duties of pastors are to arouse the conscience of the faithful to enlighten it, to act as if each of them were another Christ: "*Christ live in me*", Gal. 2,20. Christ took a firm stand against the Parisees of His day but He did not charge any of His disciples to rebike His brothers and sisters, still less excommunicate them or curse them.

The mission of the Church is essentially religious and spiritual. Christ did not give it any worldly and temporal authority; He chose His apostles and His disciples only to lay the most strict duties on them, and thus to make examples of them for the

---

[53]   Imperium is a Latin word which, in a broad sense, translates as 'power'.

flock. The early bishops or superintendents were overseers, not masters: *"for one is your Master"*, Matthew 23,8.

The Primitive Church, then was a gathering in which the first and only chief was, in the eyes of the faith, Christ Himself. Pastors and their flock formed a body and soul. This was the parish, and if any dispute arose between any of the members, it was the Church that restored peace: *"take your case to the church"*, Matthew 18,17.

Gradually bounds of Christian brotherhood and charity were formed between the various local churches, and in this way synods came into being – special and very limited synods before the idea of general councils was heard of. It is not only the idea of the true bishop, therefore, that has to be restored, but also that of the synod and the council. Because its so-called Ecumenical Council was believed to be the representation of the whole Church, the Roman Catholic jurisdiction was made universal and absolute jurisdiction, to which was soon joined the priviledge of infaillibiliby. The practical consequences resulting from this confusion and the numerous abuses arising from them to the detriment of the Church are well known.

We are also engaged in restoring the true conception of pastor, bishop, synod, council, ecclesiastical authority, and even infallibility, according to the precise meaning of the Scriptures and according to ancient traditions. The Constitution of the Church, they hold, is monarchical only because Christ is its only monarch; but inasmuch as it is a society composed of humans, the Church has been called from its very beginning a simple "church" and it has been regarded in its universality, since the time when the question of universality arose, as a Christian "republic". It would give a wrong idea of the early bishops to represent their action as an autocratic government, the word of St. Peter himself are opposed to that: "*oversee the flock of God not constrainedly*", 1 Peter 5,2.

The episcopal see of Rome was not long in attaining a certain priority, Rome being the capital of the empire; but it was merely a priority of honour, and not of jurisdiction. Christ did not appoint a master among His disciples. When he told Peter specially to feed His lambs and sheep, it was to restore to him the function of which he had proved unworthy, and of which he had been deprived in denying Christ. As Peter repented, he deserved to be reinstated, and he was; but it is a mistake to transform this reinstatement, as a simple apostle, into an exaltation above all the other apostles. The alteration of the Constitution of the Church was accomplished by Rome by means of grossly erroneous interpretations of texts; the policy and the ambitions of the bishops of Rome did the rest.

Such is the spirit in which we set about restoring the true conception of the Church and realizing the ecclesiastical reform claimed for such a long time "in capite and in membris".

Runion of the Christian Churches

This reform of the Church would have been very imperfect, if it had not from the beginning implied the reestablishment of union among the separate churches. It has been rightly said that "it is as difficult to see Christ behind the Church as to see the sun behind the darkness of night". From the very start of our work we have made it one of our aims to study means of reviving this union. Reconciliations have been affected among churches, and if the union has not yet been sanctioned, it is because there are still administrative obstacles to be overcome, and specially prejudices of a hierarchichal kind to be put down.

It is already apparent to all eyes that the "union" aimed at is not the "unity" which many had imagined at first; that the latter is not necessary, and that moreover it is impossible, considering the needs of various kinds which are prevalent among the nations and which form part of human nature itself. The chimera of false unity being removed, Christians will return to the real nature of spiritual union and of the "*bond of peace*" (Ephesians 4,3) which will be sufficient to form real brotherhood throughout the world.

A better understanding has already been reached as to the respects in which the Christian Churches ought to be one and those in which they ought to remain distinct and even different, in order to safeguard the autonomy of each and all. When all are one in loving one another, in working together for the social well-being, in banishing from their theology every trace of anthropomorphism and politics, in becoming more spiritually minded after the pattern of Christ and in establishing the reign of God in every individual conscience, then the union in question will be very near being declared: "*that they be one, even as we are one*", John 17,22.

RESULTS

Our action for church reform has produced results that are dogmatic, constitutional, disciplinary, liturgical and politico-ecclesiastical.

Dogmatic

Among the dogmatic results that we have already attained we may mention the following: the rejection and refutation of papal infallibility and of the pope's absolute and universal jurisdiction over the whole Church, the rejection and refutation of the other false dogmas taught by Rome in the Syllabus Errorum[54] and elsewhere; the reestablishment of the true idea of dogma, of its distinction from theological speculation; the restoration in practice of the Catholic test: "*what has been believed everywhere, always, and by everyone is Catholic*"; the ruling that purely Western and papist councils are not ecumenical councils, the latter being only seven in numbers (325-787); the declaration of the orthodoxy of the Eastern Church, called the "Church of the seven ecumenical councils" because it has no other faith than that which was taught by them; the bringing into prominence of the union of churches, which must be neither a submission to the pope nor a neglect of dogma, but the maintenance of the autonomy of each individual church in the universality of the whole Church.

---

[54] The Syllabus is about ideas condemned in 1864, by Pope Pius IX re: rights of the Church and its rapports with civil society, ethics and modern liberalism.

Constitutional

Of these results we may mention the reduction of the primacy of the pope to the simple degree of "primus inter pares" – a title which does not confer any dignity on him, but which lays on him the duty of attending more carefully than any other bishop the decisions of the Church, to which he is subordinate; the binding of the pope to renounce political vocation, and to confine himself to his essentially religious vocation; the return of the bishops to the simplicity of the early bishops, who were by no means prince-bishops, but who simply elected by the members and the clergy remained independent of the pope, and directed their dioceses in union with their synod; the re-establishment of the simple worshippers in their rights as active members of the Church, who also attend to the guarding of the Church's interests and the maintenance of its discipline; and the revival of national and autonomous churches, Catholic by the unity of their faith: "una fides, unus Christus, unum baptisma", Ephesians 4,5.

Disciplinary

Among disciplinary results are the following: the right of each individual church to judge of the manner most useful to itself of applying the canons of discipline formulated in the provincial synods and the ecumenical councils; and the right of restoring among the clergy the choice of celibacy or marriage.

Liturgical

The liturgical results are: the return of the proper idea of the sacraments, which are neither empty symbols nor means of producing grace "ex opere operato", but acts of worship in which Jesus Christ communicates His grace to well-affected souls; the revival of public penitence and the suppression of papal indugences, the celebration of worship in the nations language of each country, as well as the free gift of all religious work.

Politico-ecclesiastical

Lastly among the politico-ecclesiastical results mention may be made of the independence of individual churches towards the political command of Rome, and towards any political interference whatever, the Church being a religious society, and in no way a political society.

II

OTHER WRITINGS

1

TAKING CARE OF THE BODY AS WELL AS THE SOUL, WITH THE NATURAL HEALING METHODS LEARNT FROM THE OLD MONKS OF ST. ANTHONY, 1932

During the Crusades, a knight of noble birth, Sir Josslyn, Lord of La Mothe St. Didier, back from the East after a long captivity among the Saracens,[55] renounced his high position in the world in obedience to a vow, and with a few companions founded the Hospital Brothers of St. Anthony.[56]

Legend says that during his captivity, the noble knight learnt from the Arabia's physicians most of their skills and science in the treatment of leprosy and other diseases, hence his resolve to devote his life to the relief and cure of those unfortunate, who in Eastern Europe, were left to shift for themselves without care, victims of diseases, superstitions and ignorance.

---

[55] Saracen was a term used by the ancient Romans to refer to people who inhabited the deserts near the Roman province of Syria and who were distinct from Arabs. The term was later applied to Arab peoples and during the time of the Crusades came to be synonymous with *Muslim*.

[56] St. Anthony also spelled Antonios. Born circa 251, Koma, near al-Minya, Heptanomis, Egypt. Died Jan. 17, 356, Dayr Mari Antonios hermitage, near the Red Sea. Feast day January 17th. Anthony was a religious hermit and one of the earliest monks, considered the founder and father of organised Christian monasticism. His rule represented one of the first attempts to codify guidelines for monastic living.

Such was the beginning of the famous Abbey of St. Anthony in Dauphiné, France,[57] which for centuries enjoyed such a fame that sick people flocked to it from all parts of Europe.

St Anthony Abbot. (251-356) WAS 105 WHEN HE DIED YET HIS SIGHT AND HEARING WAS UNIMPAIRED AND HE HAD NOT LOST A SINGLE TOOTH /

Antonite Order Fought 'St. Anthony's Fire'

Berlin.—According to an article in the *Deutche Theologische Quartalsschrift* (German theological review), the Antonite convents have played an important role in the countries of the Occident. The members of the convents devoted their efforts to the combating of St. Anthony's Fire, the name given to a blood disease that led to the rotting of the limbs. From the year 1095 on, a system of Antonite convents was built up over the whole of Europe starting from the mother convent on the Iserre. When St. Anthony's Fire faded out, other contagious disease victims were admitted for treatment.

A disease known as *St. Anthony's Fire* [58]was healed and lost its terror, thanks to the care given by the Brothers. Today can be seen the buildings and tiny villages, with their chapels where the unfortunate ones lived in quarantine.

---

[57]   The Abbey of St. Anthony was founded to house the relics of St. Anthony the Egyptian, brought from the Holy Land by Sir Josslyn. In 1289, it was entrusted to the Antonines (founded in France around 1095, become an order of regular canons in 1298 and reunited in 1777 with the Hospitaller Order of St. John of Jerusalem (Order of Malta). At the late 19th century, the abbey was erected a major monastery of the Canons Regular of the Immaculate Conception, with Dom Adrien Grea (1828-1917) as Father Abbot.

[58]   St. Anthony's Fire, is a name given to two afflictions;
   i)   Erysipelas. A streptococcal bacteria, which if it enters a wound causes red patches on the face spreading across the cheeks and nose. Causes pimple which burst then crust over; and
   ii)   Ergotism, caused by Ergot a toxin created by fungal infection of rye. When the contaminated rye enters the human food chain, it can cause infections that lead to gangrene, and even death.

Early in life I had the priviledge to join the Brotherhood of St. Anthony (the Antonians) and to learn from the old monks their methods of healing, the herbs used in the preparation of their remedies, and for the past 25 years, in different States of the Union, I have been practicing as herbalist doctor. And everywhere I have used with unqualified success the great medicine of the Brotherhood, the *Toxin Eliminator*.[59]

In ancient times, the pilgrims in search of health were turning their eyes towards the Shrine of St. Anthony, its monks and its healing herbs.

Today, the last of the Brothers is giving to the New World, to a suffering humanity, the same care, the same remedies that took the Brotherhood centuries to discover and bring to perfection.[60]

---

[59]   The *toxin eliminator* purges yeast and parasites from the gastrointestinal tract, relieves constipation, colds, flu, allergies, weight problems, sinusitis, poor vision, impaired memory, stress, back & muscle aches, breath & body odours and skin problems. It contains a blend of: Artemesia Annua extract, Grapefruit Seed Extract, Caprylic Acid, Alfalfa (flower, leaf, sprouts), Dandelion (root), Comfrey (leaf, root), Buchu (leaf), Cat's Claw (inner bark, root) Chaparral (leaf), Astragalus (root).

[60]   Plants were used by the Hospitallers of St. Anthony for the preparation of ointments, poultices and decoctions, made with wine, honey or barley flour.

2

I CONGRATULATE AND ADMIRE YOU

Letter to Bishop Rene Vilatte, 1914

I am always interested to read your writings because I admire your desire to take the Gospels literally.

The world has abandoned Jesus for materialism and see where we are. A return to God is imperative otherwise our poor humanity will suffer a blackout.

In the latest issue of The Christian Witness it is written that Catholics believe in papal supremacy. It is on this that I wanted to protest because our fathers did not believe in it and they bristled at this Roman invention. Since the Apostolic times, it was believed that it is the Universal Church represented in its councils, which is infallible. The Ultramontanes,[61] heirs to the traditions and grandeur of the Roman Empire, are responsible for this change and they made Rome the center of Christianity.

---

[61]   Ultramontanism is a religious philosophy within the Roman Catholic Church that places strong emphasis on the prerogatives and powers of the Pope. It may consist in asserting the superiority of Papal authority over the authority of the local bishop. The term originates from the Middle Ages: when a non-Italian man was elected to the papacy, he was said to be *papa ultramontano*, that is, a Pope from beyond the mountains (referring to the Alps). Foreign students at Italian universities were also referred to as *ultramontanes*. *http://en.wikipedia.org/wiki/Ultramontanism*

At the councils of Constance and Basel,[62] where were assembled freely the vast majority of the bishops of Europe, it was decided, under the old doctrine, that the Council is above the pope; that he could be deposed for a cause, etc. This is the true doctrine of the Universal Church. The Orientals would have been able to subscribe to it, and this would have ended the schism of the Church. But the haughty, insolent and tenancy old Roman spirit, did not consider itself beaten. There were maneuvers to deify the pope as they did with Caesar. If the great Bossuet[63] was not ranked among the doctors of the Church it is because of his Gallicanism.[64]

---

[62]   The Council of Basel in 1431 renewed the decree *Sacrosancta* of the Council of Constance (1414–18), which declared that a general council draws its powers from God and that even the pope is subject to a council's direction.
http://www.britannica.com/EBchecked/topic/54798/Council-of-Basel

[63]   Jacques-Bénigne Bossuet (1627–1704) was a French bishop and theologian. As the king insisted on his clergy making an anti-papal declaration, he got leave to draw it up, and made it as moderate as he could. And when the pope declared it null and void, he set to work on a gigantic *Defensio Cleri Gallicani*, published after his death.
http://en.wikipedia.org/wiki/Jacques-Benigne_Bossuet

[64]   A doctrine originated in France (the term derives from "Gaul"), Gallicanism teaches that popular civil authority (monarchs' authority or State's authority) over the Catholic Church is comparable to that of the Pope's. Gallicanism is a rejection of ultramontanism; it is akin to a form of Anglicanism but is nuanced, however, in that it downplays the authority of the Pope in the Church without denying that there are some authoritative elements to the office associated with being *primus inter pares* (first among equals).
http://en.wikipedia.org/wiki/Gallicanism

In similar times, St. Bernard and his monks[65] converted the Barbarians. Closer to us, St. Francis of Assisi started a movement[66] that still exists today.

I pray that the Lord bless you and give you the strength to accomplish all that you propose to do for the good of mankind and for the coming of the kingdom of God on this poor land.

---

[65] Bernard of Clairvaux (1090–1153) was a French abbot and the primary builder of the reforming Cistercian order. In the year 1128, he assisted at the Council of Troyes, at which he traced the outlines of the Rule of the Knights Templar.

[66] The Franciscan movement began in the year 1208, when Francis of Assisi, having lived two years as a penitent (one who seeks to reform his life and draw closer to God through daily life and works) was joined by a few like-minded followers.

3

FREE, CATHOLIC AND GALLICAN

Poem written in 1915

We the old Gallicans,

Despite the Vatican Council,

Uphold the Catholic faith

One, holy, apostolic,

Which our fathers: the Bossuet, Dupanloup...[67]

Defended with a jealous zeal

Against the arrogant pretensions

Of the Roman prelates and clergy.

She was beautiful the Church of the Gauls,[68]

With Martin of Tours,[69] whose zeal and preaching

---

[67] Félix Antoine Philibert Dupanloup (1802–1878) was elected to the French Academy in 1854, and made bishop of Orléans in 1849. Both before and during the First Vatican Council, he opposed the definition of the dogma of papal infallibility as inopportune.

[68] The Gauls were a Celtic people living in Gaul, the region roughly corresponding to what is now France, Belgium and North Italy, from the Iron Age through the Roman period. http://en.wikipedia.org/wiki/Gauls

[69] Martin of Tours (Savaria, Pannonia (now Szombathely, Hungary), 316–397, in Candes-Saint-Martin, Gaul) was a bishop whose shrine became a famous stopping-point for pilgrims on the road to Santiago de Compostela. http://en.wikipedia.org/wiki/Martin_of_Tours

Destroyed paganism; Dionysius,[70] Irenaeus,[71] Hilary,[72]
Honorat,[73] Gilles,[74] Remi,[75] Ceasarius,[76] Vincent of Lerins,
St. Cloud,[77] Genevieve,[78] Bernard, Hugues,[79] St. Louis
And a legion of saints, doctors, martyrs and confessors.

---

[70] A Roman missionary sent into Gaul, St. Dionysius fixed his see at Paris. He seems to have suffered in the persecution of Valerian in 272, though some moderns defer his death to the beginning of the reign of Maximian Herculeus, who resided chiefly in Gaul from 286 to 292.

[71] Saint Irenaeus (+202) was Bishop of Lugdunum in Gaul, then a part of the Roman Empire (now Lyons, France). He was an early church father and his writings were formative in the early development of Christian theology. http://en.wikipedia.org/wiki/Irenaeus

[72] Hilary (300–368) was Bishop of Poitiers and is a Doctor of the Church. He was sometimes referred to as the "Hammer of the Arians" (Latin: *Malleus Arianorum*) and the "Athanasius of the West." http://en.wikipedia.org/wiki/Hilary_of_Poitiers

[73] St. Honorat (370-430) founded the Abbey of Lerins (400-410). He was the Bishop of Arles (427-430). His feast is on January 16.

[74] Gilles Hermit was born in Athens and lived in Provence in the 17th century. In the Paris area, his name is often associated with that of Saint Loup of Sens, also called Saint Leu, because their feasts are celebrated on the same day, September 1st.

[75] St. Remi was Bishop of Reims and Apostle of the Franks, (437–533). On 24 December 496 he baptised Clovis I, King of the Franks. This baptism, leading to the conversion of the entire Frankish people. http://en.wikipedia.org/wiki/Saint_Remigius

[76] St. Caesarius, bishop of Arles (470-542), has found ways of preaching the Gospel in the context of barbarous times. He was more apostle that prelate, preoccupied only to convey the Christian heritage.

[77] Saint Cloud (522–560) was the son of King Chlodomer of Orleans. He was raised in Paris by his grandmother, Saint Clotilde. He renounced all claims to the throne, and lived as a hermit.

[78] St Genevieve (419/422-502/512) is the patron saint of Paris.

[79] St Hugues, Bishop of Grenoble, 1053-1132.

St. Louis venerating the Crown of Thorns

She was beautiful the Church of France,
The Church of Christ's main branch,
Her priests, her schools, her cathedrals
And all with her in Christendom, were equal.
At Constance, was affirmed the freedom of the churches
And the Roman pontiff was primus inter pares.
In the East and the West, so was the tradition
Continued to this day by the beautiful Church of France.

In these dark and terrible days,

Deep reflections are possible

Between our governments, those of the enemy[80]

And the Court of Rome. But the latter denies

The representative power of the Catholic Church.

From the beginning she was democratic.

Democratic she remained in the East.

The same she should be again in the West.

To his church, Christ has promised his presence,

Not to a person whom fortune rises above kings and

governments, who believes to command, even to the elements.

The Caesars of Rome, in an identical manner,

Proclaimed, for all to envy, their deific powers.

But despite the wrath of the Vatican,

We remain Free, Catholic and Gallican.

---

[80] He is alluding to World War I (WWI) or First World War (called at the time the Great War): a major war centered on Europe that began in the summer of 1914. The assassination on 28 June 1914 of Archduke Franz Ferdinand of Austria by a Yugoslav nationalist was the proximate trigger of the war. On 28 July, the conflict opened with the Austro-Hungarian invasion of Serbia, followed by the German invasion of Belgium, Luxembourg and France; and a Russian attack against Germany. The fighting ended in November 1918. This conflict involved all of the world's great powers. More than 70 million military personnel, including 60 million Europeans, were mobilised in one of the largest wars in history. More than 9 million combatants were killed. It was the second deadliest conflict in Western history. http://en.wikipedia.org/wiki/World_War_I

4

NATIONAL CHURCHES DOMINATED BY THE ROMAN CURIA AND BEING SUPPRESSED, 1916

The tradition of the Gallican Church is as old as that of the Roman Church but it has not been illustrated by tombs and relics of apostles.

Ultramontanes, steeped in the traditions of the Roman Empire, used the Christian religion to perpetuate their domination over the world. Until the 9th century, the bishops of Rome were the patriarchs of the West. They envied the prelates of the imperial city, Constantinople, and feared that they usurp their place in the Church. This place was not a supremacy but a primacy of honor. It was awarded in the 5th century by the Fathers of the Church, not because the Bishop of Rome had, at the time, a higher titer (successor of St. Peter, infallible, etc.), but because he was bishop of the oldest city of the empire. The primacy was given to him by the council.

It is in the East that the Church had its beginning; that it grew and developed. This is where all matters of doctrine were discussed. It is there that the great councils were held, under the protection of the emperors, and the Bishop of Rome was invited as the others.

The East was rich, civilized, nice. Its cities were centers of culture. The West was divided into many little barbarian kingdoms with an ignorant clergy, except for some communities.

In the 9th century, Charlemagne has changed the history of the West and the Church by making the Bishop of Rome a sovereign prince with an army, coining money and signing treaties with the kings, his neighbors. Charles was a great warrior but was unaware of the history and theology, and Roman prelates made him sign the Donation of Constantine (since identified as false),[81] which restores the provinces and the city of Rome to the head of the Church. From there originate the Roman claims and the Great Schism. Materialism has invaded the Latin Church.

---

[81] The *Donation of Constantine* is a forged Roman imperial decree by which the emperor Constantine I supposedly transferred authority over Rome and the western part of the Roman Empire to the pope. During the Middle Ages, the document was often cited in support of the Roman Church's claims to spiritual and earthly authority. Italian humanist Lorenzo Valla is credited with first exposing the forgery with solid philological arguments, although doubts on the document's authenticity had already been cast by his times. Scholars have since dated the forgery between the Eighth and the Ninth Century. http://en.wikipedia.org/wiki/Donation_of_Constantine

IOANNES X.
Sedit an.15 mens.
Romanus anni 912
Obyt an.928.

Everything was modeled on the empire, its greatness and its baseness, and we saw a helmeted and cuirassed Pope (John X) lead his troops in the assault.[82]

Two movements, two basilicas, show the gulf that exists between the ideology of the Greeks and that of the Romans. The Greek dedicated to the deity Wisdom (Hagia Sophia) the most beautiful temple in the world. The Roman, friend of brute force and power, dedicated to St. Peter, the holder of the keys, the largest building in the world.

While the Latin Church was getting rich and established its control over the illiterate and semi-barbarian people of the West, the Eastern churches have disappeared one after the other... And

---

[82] John X, Pope from 914 to 928, was deacon at Bologna when he attracted the attention of Theodora, the wife of Theophylact, Count of Tusculum, the most powerful noble in Rome, through whose influence he was elevated first to the see of Bologna and then to the archbishopric of Ravenna. In direct opposition to a decree of council, John X was, at the instigation of Theodora, promoted to the papal chair as the successor of Pope Lando (913–914). He endeavoured to secure himself against his temporal enemies through a close alliance with Theophylact and Alberic, then governor of the duchy of Spoleto. In December 915 John X granted the imperial crown to Berengar of Friuli (915–924), and with the assistance of the forces of all the princes of the Italian peninsula, he took the field in person against the Saracens, over whom he gained a great victory on the banks of the Garigliano. John X perished as a result of the intrigues of Marozia, daughter of Theodora. http://en.wikipedia.org/wiki/Pope_John_X

after the fall of Constantinople,[83] we can truly say that Rome has become the only major Christian center. With Hildebrand [84] and others, the papacy was established and the primacy of the first see became supremacy and infallibility in 1870.

B. GREGORIVS VII Soanensis Bo-
niti filius, creat die 23 Aprilis ann.1073.
Sedit an.12 mens i. Obijt die 24 Maij
an.10 8 5 Vac Sed. an.i.

Step by step, with tenacity and following a plan drawn in advance, the Roman Curia, through its alliances with the princes, came to suppress the national churches.

---

[83]   The Fall of Constantinople was the capture of the capital of the Byzantine Empire, which occurred after a siege by the Ottoman Empire, under the command of Sultan Mehmed II, against the defending army commanded by Emperor Constantine XI. The siege lasted from Friday, 6 April 1453 until Tuesday, 29 May 1453 (according to the Julian Calendar), when the city was conquered by the Ottomans. The Fall of Constantinople marked the end of the Byzantine Empire. http://en.wikipedia.org/wiki/Fall_of_Constantinople

[84]   Hildebrand of Sovana was Pope, under the name Gregory VII, from April 22, 1073, until his death in 1085. He was at the forefront of evolutionary developments in the relationship between the Emperor and the papacy during the years before becoming pope. He twice excommunicated Henry IV, who in the end appointed the Antipope Clement III to oppose him in the political power struggles between church and Empire. Hailed as one of the greatest of the Roman pontiffs, he was despised by many for his expansive use of papal powers. Joseph McCabe describes him as a "rough and violent peasant, enlisting his brute strength in the service of the monastic ideal which he embraced." http://en.wikipedia.org/wiki/Pope_Gregory_VII

5

THE CALL OF THE AMERICAN CATHOLIC CHURCH

Presentation made at Saint David Chapel, Chicago.
Mentioned in the <u>Chicago Tribune</u> of Sunday, May 20, 1917

In the United States there is slowly growing, silently, but steadily, the religious movement known as the American Catholic Church (A.C.C.). Its Orders are unchallenged, its ritual is that of the ages, its faith loyally Catholic, yet it is outside Papal obedience. It is a living Christian Church with a great future, small as it now is. Aside from this distinctly national A.C.C., there is no other, neither can such be brought out of the foreign religious types that abound on American soil.

There is no such a thing as an American Christianity. What of Christianity we have is an importation. The Rt. Rev. Dr. Anderson, Bishop of the Protestant Episcopal Church of Chicago, [85] declares: "We have imported certain national types of

---

[85]   Charles Palmerston Anderson (1865-1930) was the 17th Presiding Bishop of the Episcopal Church. He was born in Kemptville, Ontario. In 1900, he was elected Bishop Coadjutor of the Episcopal Diocese of Chicago and became diocesan bishop in 1905 on the death of William Edward McLaren.

.

Christianity which took their form and shape in other lands, an Italian Christianity from Italy, Lutheranism from Germany, Anglicanism from England, Presbyterianism from Scotland, Orientalism from Asia Minor", and then asks: "Is there nothing to look forward to except the permanent establishment of foreign types on American soil?" Describing the religion of America, the same prelate concludes: "It is a heterogeneous conglomeration of imported traditions", and asks: "Is there not to be a Catholicism that will express the religious life of America as Americanism expresses her national life?" To these fundamentally important questions the A.C.C. is the affirmative reply.

A National Church, in the Catholic sense, is a Church which holds the Catholic faith: but which, so far as Catholic orders permit, adapts its organization in matters not involving its catholicity to suit the feelings and the wishes and tastes of the people among whom it ministers.[86] People will repose trust in a church that fosters the soul of their own nation... Now is the time to set ourselves to the noble task of establishing a home religion, that is also, Catholic.

The American people are not opposed to a pure Catholicism. No one is. But since the only form of Catholicism they have known is that which has been presented to them by foreign nations, often

---

[86] The Church Times of March 2, 1917.

seriously tainted with zeal for place and power, they have had no choice between accepting a false Catholicism or wholly rejecting the true.

National Churches are a matter of simple history. They are not incompatible with the Catholic religion. Yet we are told that the Church cannot be National and Catholic at one and the same time. Earth's multitude are of many nations, but one blood. Similarly the Church is of one faith though set up among many nations, all under the supreme headship of Christ.

In common with all religious bodies in the United States the A.C.C. claims no legal status that is not theirs. However, by its entire aloofness from politics, its complete indifference to money (none of its clergymen receives salary), its independence of Rome, Canterbury, Moscow and any other foreign power, its loyalty to the accepted faith of undivided Christendom, its unassailable Catholicity, its stedfast and frank loyalty to the American constitution, and by its sole desire and purpose to lead Americans to a spurned of forgotten Christ by believing and practising Christianity as it was in the days of the Apostles and early disciples would call to itself the attention of thoughtful people who are concerned by the general apparent break-down of organized Christianity in this country (as in all others), and are looking for a new means of religious appeal to those who are living without the blessing of the Gospel of Christ Jesus, the Lord.

Never was there a fairer vision, never a more glorious opportunity than those which lie before the A.C.C.

Nothing is more certain than this – the future lies, not with Protestantism nor with Romanism, but with a Catholicity which is fashioned after the primitive model, and dares to bring forth out its treasury things new as well as old.

It is to be hoped that the close of the war will be coincident with the destruction of every form of autocracy spiritual as well as temporal.

6

I ACCEPT THE PRESIDENCY OF THE A.C.C.

Letter to Father W. Sullivan, July 15, 1940

My dear Chancellor:

I just received your kind letter and you may imagine my surprise in reading its content. I never had such an ambition and I feel like saying that you must be running out of timber to call me for such an office. But after deep thoughts and prayers to the Holy Spirit for divine guidance, and considering your quasi insistence in your letter, plus our small flock, I feel duty bond to accept your invitation, trusting in your help and wisdom.

Impressions and Conditions

I was trained as a Canon Regular of St. Augustine in the Roman Church and I am chagrined to see that among our clergy many smoke, drink, have a good living, etc. It looks as if there is nothing ecclesiastical in their behavior, except perhaps the clergy shirt.

If we want to live as a body, we must inoculate more discipline - or *esprit de corps* - among our candidates for Holy Orders. They must be investigated and tried. Under my leadership there will be no strangers, ordained in three days, from whom we never hear after. This should never happen! All sorts of troubles spring from such an abuse.

Let us pray for the Holy Spirit's inspiration and guidance.

APPENDIX

1

Dr. Lindlahr Nature Cure Approach & Sanitorium

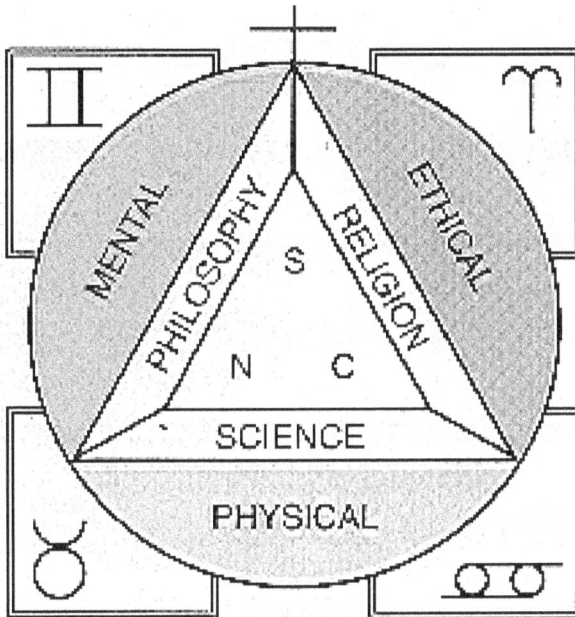

Dr. Lindlahr's approach is represented with symbols that were the concise and comprehensible summation of knowledge at that time, and formed a basis for further investigations. [87] He was merely putting several comprehensive ideas involving time, space and

---

[87] Information taken from www.NatureCure.Co.Uk

human affairs into the form of a "diagram". Here are its salient points:-

The SQUARE

This represents the "square of matter" as it was understood in the earliest times. The marking at each corner were the ancient conventional symbols for "Earth", "Air", "Fire" and "Water." Just as present day science is establishing that all matter is composed of a very small number of fundamental forms of energy, so the ancients postulated these four "elements" as the basis of their universe.

The Square is not complete, but is represented only by the four "Cornerstones." This denotes that, although our knowledge of matter may be incomplete, it is as yet sufficient to serve as the foundation for the next structure.

The CIRCLE

This <u>circle of consciousness</u> rest upon the cornerstones, but is not bounded by them. In other words, our consciousness is not restricted by or to material things: there are no limits to its expansion in space or time.

The three major conscious concepts of human existence are the physical, the mental and the ethical. Of these, the first two are relatively simple to understand, but the third may call for a little explanation. Every individual, whether he is a 'good mixer' or a hermit, is essentially part of the community. As part of the community he exhibits a group behaviour, which is in many ways totally different from his behaviour as a separate individual. To remain healthy it is essential for the individual to be helpful and friendly towards his neighbours and to the other living things - plant and animal - which surround him. He must be co-operative - Symbiotic. The code of behaviour which this involves if the essence of ethics.

From the three major aspects arise three faces of a pyramid.

The TRIANGLE

This represents the upward extension - "creative thought"- from these sectors. From the physical arises **Science**, from the mental arises **Philosophy**, and from the ethical **Religion**.

The pyramid formed by these sides of human philosophy is truncated; it reaches a small "platform" indicating the stage we have reached in our journey to the apex. This platform is labelled with the initials of the school of Nature Cure.

The CROSS

According to Dr. Lindlahr, the meaning and purpose of evolution is the completion of the co-ordination of theses studies and activities, Nature Cure occupying the highest level attained in the coordination of Science, Philosophy and Religion. Very important, however, is the figure at the top of the symbol - the "cross of Lorraine," which in ancient symbology was a formalised tree, representing continual growth and progress.

LINDLAHR SANITORIUM

In 1914, Dr. Henry Lindlahr bought 8 acres of the former Lathrop estate in Elmhurst, Illinois to establish the Lindlahr Sanitarium so that patients might receive "Nature Cure" in a country atmosphere. The sanitarium was in existence from 1914 to 1928.

The treatments included a vegetarian diet, exercise, hydrotherapy, manipulation, sunbathes and airbathes. Brochures for the sanitarium stated no drugs, serums or surgery. The reason Henry Lindlahr became a doctor was because he was a diabetic. He eventually cured his diabetes and lost 40 pounds; therefore, he devoted his life to being a doctor who didn't use medications.

Lindlahr Sanitarium was located on the south side of St. Charles Road between Cottage Hill Avenue and Prospect Avenue. The property eventually expanded to include an administration building; an annex, which had bedrooms, baths, parlors, porches, and the main treatment room; bungalows; and,

A Few of the Happy Teachers on the Road to Health

FACTS
That Speak
Louder Than Words

The *Only* Road to Health

DRESSED the wound but God healed it," said a great and wise physician. In this he merely expressed what all true healers ultimately perceive—that only Nature can heal.

Nature can heal even when all else has failed. For, assuredly, the wondrous power which built these marvelous bodies of ours can also heal them when the need arises. Nature healed the hurts and ills of primitive man ages before the dawn of medical science.

But this inscrutable inner power must not be antagonized. It must not be ignorantly meddled with. This great power inherent in us all can only be fully utilized when intelligently co-operated with.

There is one institution in the world today where this principle is followed in a thoroughly scientific, logical, result-getting way.

The Lindlahr Sanitarium
AT BEAUTIFUL ELMHURST, Near CHICAGO
ADMINISTRATIVE OFFICE • DIAGNOSTIC LABORATORIES • TRANSIENT DEPARTMENT
10TH FLOOR, BUTLER BLDG.— 162 No. STATE ST.— CHICAGO, ILL.

in the summer, a tent city with screened tents with electric lights. The large, wooded grounds provided patients with plenty of room to get exercise, which was an important part of the "Nature Cure".

2
A.C.C. Protocol, 1910

We, Joseph Rene, Archbishop Vilatte, Stephen Bishop Kaminski, and Paul Bishop Miraglia, through the Apostolic Succession transmitted lawfully, validly, and canonically to us from the venerable Patriarchal See of the East, founded in Antioch by the blessed Apostle Peter himself, which, with its indisputable apostolic authority, rights and powers, has been continued without interruption unto this day – validly consecrated bishops of the Catholic Church, joined in ecclesiastical union, and canonically assembled in the same Lord, in the orthodox Catholic Cathedral of Buffalo, on this the Feast of the Circumcision of Christ commemorated in the year 1910, do hereby solemnly affirm, repeat, and declare anew, that our Faith and Teaching is the apostolic, orthodox and

catholic doctrine as it has been truly defined, confirmed, and established by the seven ecumenical councils of the undivided Church.

Moreover, in the canonical exercise of our apostolic mission and authority, and especially for the strenghtening of our faithful, and the perfecting of our ministry in the several divisions of the Western Patriarchate, viz., in America, Europe, and Africa, we accept and declare the general authority of the use of the Latin Rite. For from the Western Ritual books we are able not only to extract and teach truly and faithfully the apostolic and primitive orthodox doctrine of the Church of Christ, but also, by means of their careful explanation and use, to restore it more and more to its former exalted state.

Furthermore, we exhort with our whole heart and in boundless charity all those who call themselves Christians, to believe and hope in Christ the Incarnate Son of God and Savior, that while preserving and defending all consistent spiritual liberty which is the fruit of rigteousness, we may truly become more and more one in faith, hope, and love, offering without ceasing continual prayers and devout petitions to the compassionate and most high God, beseeching him, the eternal Father of us all, to have mercy on those who are commonly called unbelievers, materialists, and rationalists, the members of whom through the grievous circumstances of our times, are increasing more and more, and to illumine the darkness of their doubting restless minds, so that, converted and led by the Holy Spirit, they mey be restored to the communion of the Church of Christ.

Finally, let us both labor for Christian and fraternal unity, and pray ever more fervently to the Triune God imploring and hastening of that coming day which is to bring the long awaited triumph of the One, Holy, Catholic and Apostolic Church, that glorious future day when all faithful followers of the Incarnate Son of God shall become united again, one fold and one shepherd, who is the risen and ascended Christ alone.

May the Triune God, the Father, the Son, and the Holy Spirit, through the ceasless proclamation of the holy and eternal Gospel of Christ, favor and assist us in our work for his glory in the Church Militant on earth. Amen.

Given in the city of Buffalo on the day, month, and year designated above.

3

TWO TEXTS BY BISHOP VILATTE

A
What Was Catholic Once Must Be Forever, 1914

Seven time, the whole Church was represented in council to uphold the purity of faith, spread over the world, taught alike in East and West. There was only One Church ruling the world. It was the time of Undivided Christendom. At that time nobody in search of the true Catholic Church could be perplexed or doubtful. The Church was like a city on the top of a mountain, visible everywhere. You could not mistake her, you had no choice, there was no rival. This state of things continued till the great schism between East and West.

What was Catholic once must be forever. The Catholicity of the East was recognized by the West before the latter separated. But the East did not change since, consequently, its Catholicity is unassailable, as it represents the faith of Undivided Christendom, to which all Christians are bound to return, if they do not already belong to it. This is our Christian Catholic standoint, our platform. Our orthodox Old Catholic church is the true Church instituted by Christ in the West.

There is only One Church which teaches all things whatsoever Christ has commanded and to this church He commands us to convert mankind. (*Go ye therefore, and teach all nations,* Matthew 28: 19-20) and His command is of the most pressing nature, as He Himself shows in the parable of the great supper. The master not only invites his friends and acquaintances, but sends his servant "*into the highways and hedges*" and tells him to "*compel them to come in*" (Luke 14:23). Apparently He means to continue its endeavors to bring safely home the poor wanderer lost in the wilderness of unbelief, doubt, heresy and schism. The true shepherd "*goes into the mountains, and seeks the sheep which is gone astray*" (Matthew 18:12). He does not stand with folded arms, unconcerned about its fate, coolly waiting for its return, and ready not to shut the gate in its face. The true shepherd in search of the lost sheep does not ask whether he would perhaps wound the sensibilities of the stray sheep, it is enough that he knows that the sheep is not on the right way, and consequently he thinks it his duty to call back the poor wanderer, however unwilling the latter may be.

Jesus Christ, our true Shepherd, went on preaching in spite of all resistance, persecution and scorn till they nailed Him to the cross. He will protect His church and ward off the dangers threatening her within and without. *The gates of hell shall not prevail against her (Matthew 16:18).*

While this is our belief, we desire to force no one's assent. Let all human beings follow the light of their own conscience. For it is our absolute conviction it is only by so doing we can please the Great Giver of reason. We want freedom to worship God, but we demand equal freedom for all to worship or abstain from worship, to believe or to disbelieve. In other words, not mere tolerance but perfect liberty for one and all – the believer, the unbeliever, the Catholic, the agnostic, Jew, Turk and Hindu, Parsee and Buddhist, persuaded that if not in this life, then in a life to come, at some time, the TRUTH shall be so presented to the intellect that every rational soul *"shall receive the truth, and the truth shall set him free"* (John 8:32).

B
We Maintain the Faith Once For All Given to the Saints, 1910

The only historical and consistent bond of church unity is that of *"the faith once for all given to the saints"* (Jude 3), as held by the United Church of Christendom, East and West, during the period of the Seven General Councils.

We join in faith, hope and love with all churches having the Apostolic ministry and accepting the teaching of the Holy Scriptures as understood by the Fathers, Doctors and Confessors of the undivided Church. But valid ministry alone is not sufficient for Christian unity. Christians must also accept the Apostles and the Nicean Creed without addition or substraction. We likewise acknowledge the dogmatic decrees of the seven Ecumenical Councils as the fundamental basis of unity, and the consentient definitions of the councils of Bethlehem[88] and Trent[89] concerning the seven sacraments, as being a clear and concise statement of the doctrine held by the Catholic Church throughout the world.

We reject and deny the supremacy or infallibility of any patriarch or prelate who demands sole jurisdiction over the Holy Catholic and Apostolic Church of Christ.

The Monastic life among Orthodox Catholics is a devout life of sacrifice and love towards God and humans.

We do not adore the images of Jesus Christ, the Blessed Virgin Mary and the Saints but venerate them as sacred things

---

[88]   This council, which is also called Synod of Jerusalem, was convened by Greek Orthodox Patriarch Dositheos Notaras in March, 1672. It reasserted traditional Orthodox doctrines about the Real Presence of Christ in the Eucharist and its decrees received universal acceptance as an expression of the faith of the Greek Orthodox Church.

[89]   The Council of Trent was the 16th-century Ecumenical Council of the Roman Catholic Church. It is considered to be one of the Church's most important councils. It convened in Trent (then capital of the Prince-Bishopric of Trent, in the Holy Roman Empire, now in modern Italy) between December 13, 1545, and December 4, 1563. The Council defined Church teachings in the areas of Scripture and Tradition, Original Sin, Justification, Sacraments, the Eucharist in Holy Mass and the veneration of saints. By specifying Catholic doctrine on salvation, the sacraments, and the Biblical canon, the Council was answering Protestant disputes.
http://en.wikipedia.org/wiki/Council_of_Trent

representing sacred persons. We believe there is but "*One Mediator of Redemption between God and man*" (1 Timothy 2:5). But that it is a good and useful thing to invoke the Saints who are our glorified brethren, even as we invoke the prayers of our brethren on earth.

We allow no dissent in matters of faith for no one has a right to add to or take away from the faith of the Catholic Church.

The day is at end to meet the Lord, and the Spirit of God impels us to cry, *Come Lord Jesus* (1 Cor 16,22). For the prosperity of the Christian Church and for its union, let us pray constantly.

The Smaller Catechism

FOR THE USE OF

American Catholics

Compiled and Published by
THE REV. FREDERIC E. J. LLOYD, D. D.
3657 Grand Boulevard   Chicago, Ill.

The American Catholic Church is the only truly national Catholic Church in the United States. Other Catholic Churches in the United States are not American, nor do they claim to be. Its Apostolic Succession is derived from the apostolic see of Antioch of which St. Peter was the founder. Its faith is that of the undivided Holy Catholic Church before 1054. It is not Roman Catholic, neither is it Protestant—it is American, Catholic, and Apostolic.

IMPRIMATUR:

✚ *JOSEPH RENE VILATTE*

ARCHBISHOP

THE
SMALLER CATECHISM
FOR THE USE OF
AMERICAN CATHOLICS

The Sign of the Cross.

✛ In the name of the Father, and of the Son
and of the Holy Ghost. Amen.

The Our Father.

Our Father, who art in heaven! Hallowed be thy
Name. Thy kingdom come. Thy will be done on
earth, As it is in heaven. Give us this day our
daily bread. And forgive us our trespasses, As
we forgive those who trespass against us. And
lead us not into temptation; But deliver us from
evil. Amen.

The Hail Mary.

Hail, Mary, full of grace, the Lord is with thee;
blessed art thou among women, and blessed is the
fruit of thy womb, Jesus. Holy Mary, Mother of
God, pray for us sinners, now, and at the hour of
our death. Amen.

1

The Apostles' Creed.

I believe in God the Father Almighty, Creator of heaven and earth:

And in Jesus Christ his only Son our Lord, Who was conceived by the Holy Ghost, Born of the Virgin Mary, Suffered under Pontius Pilate, Was crucified, dead, and buried; He descended into hell; The third day he rose again from the dead; He ascended into heaven, And sitteth on the right hand of God the Father Almighty; From thence he shall come to judge the living and the dead.

I believe in the Holy Ghost; the holy Catholic Church; The Communion of Saints; The Forgiveness of sins; The Resurrection of the body; And the Life everlasting. Amen.

The Ten Commandments.

1.—I am the Lord thy God who brought thee out of the land of Egypt, out of the house of bondage. Thou shalt have none other gods but me. Thou shalt not make unto thyself any graven idol nor the likeness of any thing that is in heaven above, or in the earth beneath, or in the water under the earth, thou shalt not adore them nor serve them.

2.—Thou shalt not take the Name of the Lord thy God in vain.

3.—Remember that thou keep holy the Sabbath day.

4.—Honor thy father and thy mother.

5.—Thou shalt do no murder.

6.—Thou shalt not commit adultery.

7.—Thou shalt not steal.

8.—Thou shalt not bear false witness against thy neighbor.

9.—Thou shalt not covet thy neighbor's wife

10.—Thou shalt not covet thy neighbor's goods.

2

The First Commandment Commands Us—

To study to know what God has taught by attending Catechism class; to say our night and morning prayers; to make a proper use of our talents.

The First Commandment Forbids Us—

To be irreverent in Church, and especially at Holy mass; to attend places of false worship; to read bad books; to delay doing penance; to be ashamed of our religion.

II.

The Second Commandment Commands Us—

To speak with reverence of God and of the saints and of all holy things, and to keep our lawful oaths and vows.

The Second Commandment Forbids Us—

To use the name of God in a light or careless way or in anger; to tell a lie when we have taken a lawful oath to tell the truth; to take an unnecessary or rash oath; to use profane words and to curse; to try to make others curse.

III.

The Third Commandment Commands Us—

To rest from servile works, to hear Holy Mass, and receive instruction on Sundays and Holydays.

The Third Commandment Forbids Us—

To do our ordinary work by which we earn our living on Sunday unless necessity requires it.

3

IV.

The Fourth Commandment Commands Us—

To love, honor and obey our parents in all that is not sin; to support them in old age; to honor and obey the church authorities and the civil magistrates whom God has set over us in all that is not unjust.

The Fourth Commandment Forbids Us—

To be disobedient and disrespectful towards our parents, teachers and lawful superiors; to make them angry; to neglect them in their trouble and necessity.

V.

The Fifth Commandment Commands Us—

To live in peace and union with our neighbor; to respect his rights; to seek his spiritual and bodily welfare; and take proper care of our own life and health.

The Fifth Commandment Forbids—

All wilful murder, fighting, anger, hatred, revenge, and bad example.

VI. and IX.

The Sixth and Ninth Commandments Command Us—

To be pure in thought and modest in all our looks, words, and actions; to banish bad thoughts.

The Sixth and Ninth Commandments Forbid—

All immodesty with ourselves or others in dress, looks, words, or actions; to go with bad companions; the reading of bad books and papers.

4

VII

The Seventh Commandment Commands Us—

To give to all what belongs to them, and to be careful not to damage their property; to restore any stolen goods which we may have in our possession or the value of them as far as we are able; and to repair any damage we have unjustly caused.

The Seventh Commandment Forbids Us—

To take or keep unjustly what belongs to another.

The Eighth Commandment Commands Us—

To speak the truth in all things, and to be careful of the honor and reputation of every one; to repair any injury we do to the honor and reputation of our neighbor. To be loyal to our country and its institutions.

The Eighth Commandment Forbids—

All rash judgments, backbiting, slanders, carrying tales to make discord between neighbors, and lying.

The Tenth Commandment Commands Us—

To be content with what we have, and to rejoice in our neighbor's welfare.

The Tenth Commandment Forbids—

All desire to take or keep wrongfully what belongs to another.

The Confiteor.

I confess to Almighty God, to Blessed Mary ever-virgin, to Blessed Michael the Archangel, to Blessed John the Baptist, to the Holy Apostles Peter and Paul, and to all the saints, that I have sinned exceedingly in thought, word, and deed, through my fault, through my most grievous fault. Therefore I beseech the Blessed Mary ever-virgin, Blessed Michael the Archangel, Blessed John the Baptist, the Holy Apostles Peter and Paul, and all the saints, to pray to the Lord our God for me.

May the Almighty God have mercy upon me, forgive me my sins, and bring me to everlasting life. Amen.

May the Almighty and merciful Lord grant me pardon ✠ absolution, and remission of all my sins. Amen.

An Act of Faith.

O my God, I believe all the truths which thou hast revealed, because thou art the truth itself, and so thou canst neither be deceived, nor deceive us.

An Act of Hope.

O my God, I hope that through the merits of Jesus Christ thou wilt grant me everlasting life, and all the graces necessary to obtain it.

An Act of Charity or Love.

O my God, I love thee with all my heart, because thou art infinitely good. And I love my neighbor also for the love of thee.

6

An Act of Contrition.

O my God, I am heartily sorry for having sinned, because thou art infinitely good, and sin offendeth thee. Forgive me through the merits of Jesus Christ thy Son. Grant me grace never more to offend thee, and to do penance for all that is past.

Prayer for the Dead.

May the Souls of the faithful through the mercy of God rest in peace.

(It is the duty of parents to teach all that precedes to their children.)

Q. What are the chief mysteries of the Christian Religion?

A. The Creation. the Trinity, the Incarnation, the Redemption, and the Seven Sacraments.

(Let the catechist instruct orally in regard to the Creation, Trinity, the Incarnation and Redemption.)

Q. Name the Seven Sacraments?

A. Baptism, Confirmation. Holy Eucharist, Penance, Holy Orders, Matrimony, and Unction of the Sick.

Q. What is Baptism?

A. Baptism is a Sacrament which cleanses us from sin and makes us Christians.

Q. How is Baptism given?

A. By dipping the person to be baptized in water, or putting water upon the person's head, saying these words: I baptize thee in the name of the Father ✠ and of the ✠ Son, and of the ✠ Holy Ghost.

Q. What is Confirmation?

A. Confirmation is a Sacrament in which we receive the Holy Ghost to make us strong and perfect Christians.

7

Q. How does the Bishop give Confirmation?

A. He lays his hands on the heads of the persons to be confirmed, prays the Holy Ghost to come down upon them, and makes the sign of the cross on their foreheads with holy chrism.

Q. What is given in Holy Communion?

A. The true Body and Blood of Jesus Christ under the forms of bread and wine.

Q. How must we come to Communion?

A. Fasting, and after confession.

Q. What is the Sacrament of Penance?

A. Penance is the Sacrament established by Christ to remit sins committed after baptism.

Q. How many parts are there in the Sacrament of penance?

A. Two. Confession to the priest, with true sorrow for sin, and the priest's absolution.

Q. What is Holy Orders?

A. Holy Orders is the Sacrament by which bishops, priests, and deacons. are ordained and receive the power and grace to perform their sacred duties.

Q. What is the Sacrament of Matrimony?

A. It is the Sacrament which joins a Christian man and woman together as man and wife in the Church of God.

Q. What is Unction of the Sick?

A. Unction of the Sick is a Sacrament in which a sick person, through the anointing with holy oil and prayers of the priest, receives the grace of God for the healing of the soul, and often, also of the body.

8

The Commandments of the Church.

Q. What are the principal commandments of the Church?

A. (1) To hear Mass on Sundays and feasts of obligation.

(2) To fast and abstain from flesh meat on the days appointed.

(3) To go to confession at least once a year.

(4) To receive Holy Communion during Eastertide.

(5) To help support our pastors.

(6) Not to marry within the forbidden degrees.

The Three Theological Virtues.

1. Faith.
2. Hope.
3. Charity.

The Four Cardinal Virtues.

1. Justice.
2. Prudence.
3. Temperance.
4. Fortitude.

The Seven Gifts of the Holy Ghost.

1. Wisdom.
2. Understanding.
3. Counsel.
4. Spiritual Strength.
5. Knowledge.
6. True Godliness.
7. Holy Fear.

9

The Twelve Fruits of the Holy Spirit.

1. Love.
2. Joy.
3. Peace.
4. Long-suffering.
5. Gentleness.
6. Goodness.
7. Faith.
8. Meekness.
9. Patience.
10. Modesty.
11. Temperance.
12. Chastity.

The Seven Corporal Works of Mercy.

1. To feed the hungry,
2. To give drink to the thirsty.
3. To clothe the naked.
4. To harbor the stranger and needy.
5. To visit the sick.
6. To minister unto prisoners and captives.
7. To bury the dead.

The Seven Spiritual Works of Mercy.

1. To instruct the ignorant.
2. To correct offenders.
3. To counsel the doubtful.
4. To comfort the afflicted.
5. To suffer injuries with patience.
6. To forgive offences and wrongs.
7. To pray for others.

10

The Eight Beatitudes.

1. Blessed are the poor in spirit: for theirs is the kingdom of Heaven.
2. Blessed are they that mourn: for they shall be comforted.
3. Blessed are the meek: for they shall inherit the earth.
4. Blessed are they which do hunger and thirst after righteousness: for they shall be filled.
5. Blessed are the merciful: for they shall obtain mercy.
6. Blessed are the pure in heart: for they shall see God.
7. Blessed are the peacemakers: for they shall be called the Children of God.
8. Blessed are they which are persecuted for righteousness' sake: for theirs is the Kingdom of Heaven.

The Seven Mortal Sins, and the Contrary Virtues.

1. Pride.	1. Humility.
2. Covetousness.	2. Liberality.
3. Lust.	3. Chastity.
4. Envy.	4. Gentleness.
5. Gluttony.	5. Temperance.
6. Anger.	6. Patience.
7. Sloth.	7. Diligence.

Nine Ways of Sharing in the Sin of Another.

1. By counsel.
2. By command.
3. By consent.
4. By provocation.
5. By praise or flattery.
6. By concealment.
7. By partaking.
8. By silence.
9. By defence of the ill done.

11

Six Sins Against the Holy Spirit.
1. Presuming on God's mercy.
2. Despair.
3. Impugning a known truth.
4. Envy at another's good.
5. Obstinacy in sin.
6. Final impenitence.

Three Notable Duties.
1. Fasting.
2. Almsgiving.
3. Prayer.

The Three Parts of True Repentance.
1. Contrition.
2. Confession.
3. Satisfaction.

The Evangelical Counsels.
1. Voluntary Poverty.
2. Perpetual Chastity, i. e. Perpetual Virginity or Widowhood.
3. Holy Obedience.

The Four Last Things.
1. Death.
2. Judgment.
3. Heaven.
4. Hell.

The Seven Words on the Cross.
1. Father, forgive them, for they know not what they do.
2. Verily I say unto thee, Today shalt thou be with me in Paradise.
3. Woman, behold thy Son! Behold thy Mother!
4. My God, my God, why hast Thou forsaker me?
5. I thirst.
6. It is finished.
7. Father, into Thy hands I commend spirit.

12

Anima Christi.

Soul of Christ, sanctify me!
Body of Christ, save me!
Blood of Christ, inebriate me!
Water from the Side of Christ, wash me!
O Good Jesus, hear me!
Suffer me not to be separated from Thee!
From the malicious enemy defend me!
In the hour of my death, call me,
And bid me come to Thee:
That with Thy saints I may praise Thee
Forever and ever. Amen.

Subjects for Daily Meditation and Prayer.

Remember, Christian Soul, that thou hast this day, and every day of thy life,

God to glorify,
Jesus to imitate.
A soul to save.
A body to mortify.
Sins to repent of.
Virtues to acquire.
Hell to avoid.
Heaven to gain.
Eternity to prepare for.
Time to profit by.
Neighbors to edify
The world to despise.
Devils to combat.
Passions to subdue.
Death, perhaps, to suffer.
Judgment to undergo.

13

GRACE BEFORE MEALS.

Bless us, O Lord, and this food of which we are
about to partake. ✠ In the name of the Father, and of the Son, and of the Holy Ghost. Amen.

THANKS AFTER MEALS.

We give thee thanks, Almighty God, for these
and all thy benefits, thou who livest and reignest
for ever and ever. Amen. ✠ In the name of
the Father, and of the Son, and of the Holy
Ghost. Amen.

✠

'14

Poem « Fredericus Lloyd Americae Episcopus »

Fredericus Lloyd Americae(ILL.)Episcopus
ab Apostolica Sede Antiochena(Unica Petri Sede)
    Successionem Apostolicam
    Legitime repetens.
Anglicanus erat;lectus,refugitque Cathedram,
    Et Romam petiit,quam cito itemque fugit.
Antiochenam inde optavit praecingere Mitram;
    Tum dedimus nos jura sacrata Petri.
Si Americana Fides nunc vult res integra adesse
    Jungi iterum per eum Linea rupta potest.

Translation

Frederick Lloyd, you are legitimately bishop of America (Illinois) in the apostolic succession of Antioch (the only see of Peter).

You have left the Anglicans who had elected you bishop, to go to Rome and, ultimately, to join us in the communion of Antioch.

We confered on you the sacred powers going back to Peter so that faith be preserved and transmitted in America in its entirety.

+Paolo Miraglia-Gullotti, December 1915

6

Why The American Catholic Church Cannot Accept Roman Catholic Orders.

CONSIDERING that no election to the Bishopric of Rome did ever take place without execrable intrigues, scandals, or, even, murders, it is obvious that the see of Rome cannot claim an Apostolic Succession that is free from pollution. Papist historians themselves are witnesses in this behalf, and Desanctis, Consultor of the Holy Office, clearly shows from the *Annales Ecclesiastici* of Cardinal Baronius that there is ample reason for wholly rejecting the validity of the Roman Succession. Besides, continuity was absolutely destroyed by Pope Pius X. by cancelling, in a special decree, thirteen popes from the roll of Roman Bishops, some as anti-popes, some because they never even existed, as for example, Anacletus.

The doctrine of Intention in the Church of Rome is fundamentally destructive of any and all assurance in relation to sacramental Grace. This is well attested by the fact that in South America there used to be a rule that no one with a strain of native blood down to the fourth generation could be ordained to the Roman priesthood. A bishop did ordain some such young men, and when he found out that they were disqualified he declared that his intention was absent and that they were still laymen. On appeal Rome took the same view. We cannot, therefore, be certain that a single bishop or priest of the Roman Communion is validly consecrated or ordained, since the intention of their consecrators or ordainers may have been *absent*.

In the light of these facts, therefore, the Consistory of The American Catholic Church has decided that there is no true Apostolic Succession in the Church of Rome, and, further, no Bishop of the American Catholic Church will admit to her ministry any Roman Catholic priest or others whose orders have been derived from Rome, without ordination.   ✠ **PAOLO EPISCOPUS MIRAGLIA**

THE ANTIOCHEAN

UT OMNES

UNUM SINT

Vol. 1.   APRIL, 1928.   No. 4

THE PRIMATES ADDRESS AT THE HOTEL ATLANTIC, COMMUNICATED

On Monday, March the fifth the Most Reverend Fredric, Primate of the American Catholic Church, addressed by invitation, a gathering of fifty Evangelical ministers of the City of Chicago, at the Hotel Atlantic. The Primate's theme was "The aims and claims of the American Catholic Church." The address, occupied more than half-an-hour, was attentively listened to, and from the many expressions of approval made to the Primate before he left the lecture room, it made a good impression.

Dr. Lloyd pointed to the American Catholic Church as the one and only Church in the United States capable of providing a meeting-place for all the Christians (of more than three-hundred denominations) in America. Free of vested interest, without endowments, with the Missal for the Catholic and the Bible for the Evangelical, neither Fundamentalist nor Modernist her ministration to all Sorts and Conditions of Christians to come and reason together about Christian Unity is strong and sincere and intelligent. She aims to bring about Christian Unity and prays for it, by leading Christians to sanctification. The unregenerate Christian cares nothing for Christian Unity the consecrated Christian, a true believer in the Divinity of our Blessed Lord, and in the completeness of His Incarnation cares for little else. How can Christian men and women love Christ who are a variance (even denominationally) with one another!

Since she is the American Catholic Church, she is profoundly interested in the racial question. Representative of every nation under heaven are to be found in the United States, and in process of time with the help of education, these peoples will be (or ought to be) fused into a homogeneous whole. Thus the American Catholic Church aims to bring them all into her fold. Already she has successfully demonstrated that aim, and in a most practical way, caring for no one race above another. but holding all nations to be born of God and of one blood. The African has his Bishop and leader within person of the Editor of the "Antiochean," the Rt. Rev. Ernest Leopold Peterson, D. C. L., the Swede his in the Rt. Rev. Axell Fryxell, the Italian his in the Rev. Vincent E. Priscitelli, the Pole his in the Rt. Rev. Bishop Kanski and the Rev. F. I. Boryszewski, the Frenchman his in the Rt. Rev. Bishop Durand and the Rev. Dr. J. N. Bodot. and the German his in the Very Rev. W. O. Homer, D. D., D. C. L., Chancellor of the Church.

First, Catholic with her whole heart and soul, then, American, zealously devoted to the development of the American Nation in her noblest and best aspirations free from the taint of denominationalism or racialism, simple, unaffected, without prejudice caring chiefly for the salvation of the vast peoples of the Americas through Christ, and in His Church, she would melt denominationalism by the love of God, and bring all the dispersed of His flock into One, Holy, Catholic Church of America.

The Primate believed that he would carry his hearers with him when he declared that Protestantism was a spent force and that the coming time would see the triumph of Catholicism, not, to wit, of the early and purest ages of Christendom. The American Catholic Church will become the Catholic Church of and for America—no doubt of it!

THE PRIMATE'S EUROPEAN TOUR

The Primate is leaving America on the 20th of April for England, where, on the 10th of May he will be present at the annual banquet of the Intercollegiate University, in London. His Grace will ordain five or more gentlemen to the sacred priesthood, who will be thereafter associated with Canon Churchill Sibley in developing, and carrying on the work of our beloved Church in the British Islands.

Before returning to America, the Primate will voyage to Norway and Sweden and other parts of Scandinavia, and he hopes to be home again early in August.

EASTER

Easter Sunday is the first Sunday after the first full moon after the vernal equinox, the first day of the Spring, or the 21st of March. It is upon this date that the variable part of the Church Calendar principally depends.

8

FIAT LUX : COMMON SENSE AND LOGIC, 1928

A summary

The purpose of the brochure is to bring the Franco-Americans[90] to join Bishop Durand's church (A.C.C.).

The text says that Rome has led religion out of its original meaning. It advocates staying true to the catholicity of the time before papism[91] was invented in the 9th century, in the *false decretals*, [92] and which took shape in the 16th century, under the influence of Bellarmine[93] and the Jesuits. True to the catholicity

---

[90] Particularly those who, under the auspices of the Woonsocket newspaper La Sentinelle (1925-1928), were opposing Bishop William Hickey.

[91] The term means one who supports Papal authority over all Christians. http://en.wikipedia.org/wiki/Papist

[92] The False Decretals--also called the Decretals of Pseudo-Isidore because their compilers passed as St. Isidore of Seville, purports to be a collection of decrees of councils and decretals of popes (written replies on questions of ecclesiastical discipline) from the first seven centuries. The collection contains (1) the letters of the popes preceding the Council of Nicaea (325) from Clement I to Miltiades, all of which are forgeries; (2) a collection of the decrees of councils, most of which are genuine, though the forged Donation of Constantine is included; (3) a large collection of letters of the popes from Sylvester I (died 335) to Gregory II (died 731), among which there are more than 40 falsifications. http://www.uv.es/EBRIT/micro/micro_202_86.html

[93] Robert Bellarmine (1542-1621), a Jesuit, published a large number of writings, of which *Disputationes controversiis Christianae fidei*, which gives a clear and systematic rationale for the position of the Roman Pontiff. Became a cardinal in 1599 and was archbishop of Capua from 1602 to 1605. He returned to Rome as adviser to the Pope.

that gave to Peter and his successors the primacy of honor and charity, not the infallible jurisdiction over all the faithful individually and collectively.

In this regard, is mentioned the speech of Josip Strossmayer (1815-1905), Bishop of Diakovar, Croatia, at the 1st Vatican Council, on June 2, 1870. The text recalls his conclusions, based on the testimony of Christ, of the early Church, of Saints Peter and Paul, and of the Church Fathers: (1) Jesus gave his apostles the same power as Peter; [94] (2) they did not recognized him as vicar of Christ and the Church's infallible teacher; (3) Peter never believed to be pope or acted as if he was; (4) the councils of the first four centuries have given the see of Rome a certain primacy because the city became the capital of the Roman Empire, but it is a primacy of honor, not of jurisdiction; (5) the church Fathers have understood the famous passage *Thou art Peter and upon this rock I will build my Church* (Mat. 16:18) to mean not that the Church is built on the apostle Peter (super Petrum), but rather on the rock of the faith he professed (super petram).

---

[94] We find this affirmation in Article 1 of our Statement of Faith (Duval, Wisconsin, 1889), which is reproduced in Fiat Lux, p. 36. It reads: « *The Gospels tell us that the apostles had the same power and authority. This is not to Peter alone that Jesus gave the power to bind and loose, but to all the apostles* ».

Are also mentioned: the speech Henri des Houx (1848-1911) [95] made in Paris after his resignation as editor of the Journal de Rome, and texts of St. Cyprian,[96] St. Augustine, [97] St. Vincent of Lerins, Pierre Harispe,[98] Msgr. d'Hulst [99]...

H. des Houx

---

[95]   When he was Director of the League of the Catholics of France, he asked the predecessor of Bishop Durand (+R. Vilatte) to help structure the movement of the *Cultuelles* (organizations that support religious worship) called for by the 1905 French Law on the Separation of the Churches and the State.

[96]   Thascius Caecilianus Cyprianus (+258), Bishop of Carthage (North Africa), defended the prerogatives of the bishops against papal centralism in his De Catholicae Ecclesiae and in his correspondence with Pope Stephen I.

[97]   Augustine lived from 354 to 430 and was bishop of Hippo in North Africa. For him, the Church finds its unity in the mutual charity of its members, and is holy because of its goal, not its members. They inherited a moral evil (original sin) from which only divine grace can save them.

[98]   A specialist of Lamenais, Harispe wrote the article *The pariahs of the priesthood* and *Cardinal Mathieu* in La Nouvelle Revue, 1910-1914.

[99]   Bishop Maurice Le Sage d'Hauteroche d'Hulst (1841-1896) founded in 1875 the Institut Catholique de Paris, which he led from 1881 until his death. He was organizer of international scientific conferences, Lenten preacher at Notre-Dame de Paris (1891-1896) and deputy of Brest (1892). He displayed a great activity in several areas related to faith apologetics philosophy, scripture, spiritual ministry and political responsibility.

Blaise Pascal

We must return to the faith of our fathers, to Gallicanism, says the text. *Let there be no mistake: with Bossuet, Fenelon,* [100] *Pascal,*[101] *and all the clergy of France, our fathers believed that the pope holds his spiritual authority from the Church and that he may be removed from office if he is proved unworthy*.

The brochure denounces the Roman Curia as largely composed of men taking orders for the sole purpose of living well.[102] Following the example of their leaders, many would seek to hoard and to satisfy their carnal passions.[103] The A.C.C. has solutions for these ills. It allows priests to marry, in accordance with the practice of the Ancient Church. By imposing celibacy, Rome would doom the clergy to an immoral life. "*Many lewd and drunken priests are found in the U.S.A., in Canada and*

---

[100] Francois de Salignac de La Mothe-Fenelon (1651-1715), bishop of Cambrai and writer, was part of the circle that surrounded Bossuet, the spokesman of the French episcopate and the writer of the Gallican Articles.

[101] Blaise Pascal (1623-1662), French scholar and theologian. He said that the Pope hates and fears the scientists who are not subjected to him by vow, and he stood against the future dogma of papal infallibility. Miguel de Unanumo, « La foi pascalienne », Revue de Métaphysique et de Morale, no 2 (1923), pp. 345-349.

[102] Fiat Lux, p. 35.

[103] Idem, p. 30.

elsewhere." [104] It is reasonable that the priests earn their living from the Altar, but not that they use it to get rich on the backs of people: " *Tend the flock of God according to His will; nor for sordid gain*" (1 Peter 5:2). In Bishop Durand's church, *parish finances are controlled by the faithful. They have the entire administration*." [105]

If we want to be good Catholics, the thing to do is return to the Catholicism of the early days of the Church. Back to drink from the pure waters of the Church founded by Christ and based in Antioch. [106] She has survived in an apostolic succession unbroken from St. Peter until Patriarch Ignatius Peter III. The episcopate and ministry of the A.C.C. originates from him.[107]

---

[104]   Fiat Lux, p. 33-34.

[105]   Idem, p. 41.

[106]   Idem, p. 38.

[107]   The Syriac Orthodox Church holds him as the 116th successor to St. Peter at Antioch. He became Patriarch in 1872, in Jerusalem and died in 1894, in Turkey. In a bull issued 31 December 1891, the patriarch authorized the consecration of Msgr. Rene Vilatte, first bishop of the church and predecessor of Bishop Durand. The ceremony was held in Colombo (Sri Lanka) on May 29, 1892.

9

CRUSADER

Published in the interest of the American Catholic Church

VOL. I   November 1936   No. ②

OFFICIAL STATEMENT

The American Catholic Church was incorporated under the laws of the State of Illinois in 1915 which gives it legal status wherby it is recognized as a religious corporation and has the right to acquire and hold property.

It is Catholic because it accepts the Catholic Creeds and also accepts the Dogmas of the Seven General Councils which are accepted by the whole Catholic Church, both East and West.

It is Apostolic because it possesses the Apostolic Succession, derived through the Ancient Syrian Church by favor of the Syrian Patriarch of Antioch, Ignatius Peter the Third and adheres to the Apostolic Teaching and Tradition.

The American Catholic Church administers the Seven Sacraments which the Whole Church, East and West regard as the ordinary means of Santifying Grace.

The American Catholic Church rejects the doctrine of the Papal Church, which proclaims the Bishop of Rome as the Universal Bishop of Christendom, along with the assertion of his infallibility and the doctrine of indulgences. It gives no fealty to any foreign Bishop or Potentate but is autonomous and self governing.

It holds that the Cultus of the Blessed Virgin has been exaggerated by the teaching and practice of the Roman Catholic Church, out of all proportion to the truth as embodied in the Article of Faith relating to belief in the Communion of Saints.

The American Catholic Church does not forbid her clergy to marry but considers it lawful for them to marry if they choose to do so.

It is the aim of the American Catholic Church to create in the United States, a National Catholic Church for Americans who desire a Church truly Catholic and Apostolic without respect of race or color, with a Liturgy in the English tongue which happens to be the language of these United States.

　　　　　　　　　　　　✠ D.C. Hinton, D.D.
　　　　　　　　　　　　Archbishop - Primate

10

Amendment to the Articles of Incorporation of A.C.C.

PENNSYLVANIA 332 RPR 29 43 25 DATE 4-29-43

STATE OF ~~ILLINOIS~~ } ss. FILING FEE $

County of PHILADELPHIA } *Edward...ed.* CLERK ~~Wo 2~~

I hereby certify that at /the Second Quarterly Meeting ~~~~ of the members of the

Board of Trustees of the American Catholic Church, a corporation of the State of Illinois

held on the Twenty-first day of April A. D. 1943, at Two o'clock P M., pursuant to the rules of said corporation, the following resolution was adopted, in accordance with the By-Laws of said corporation:

Resolved : That in compliance with the provisions of the laws of the State of

Illinois under the Articles of Incorporation granted by said state which governs

this Board of Trustees it being necessary to establish in the records of the

Secretary of State of the State of Illinois the proper address within the state

of the American Catholic Church the Secretary is hereby instructed to file with

the said Secretary of State an Amendment to the Articles of Incorporation of the

American Catholic Church which shall read as follows - " The principle address of

the corporation shall be 6417 Forest Preserve Drive in the City of Chicago . "

Very Reverend Benedict Moyer

Vary Reverend Benedict Moyer

SECRETARY

PENNSYLVANIA

STATE OF ~~ILLINOIS~~ } ss.

County of PHILADELPHIA }

I, William Siple being duly sworn, declare on oath that I am

President of the corporation mentioned in the foregoing certificate, and that the statements therein are true in substance and in fact.

In witness whereof, I have hereunto set my hand and caused the seal of

said Corporation to be affixed, this 26TH

day of APRIL A. D. 19 43

(Corporate Seal Here)

William Siple

PRESIDENT

Subscribed and sworn to before me this 26TH day of APRIL

A. D. 19 43

Ira D. Cochran

NOTARY PUBLIC

NOTARY PUBLIC

My Commission Expires May 6, 1944

7 2d 43

11
Statement re: Bishop Durand

MGR CASIMIR F. DURAND (1879-1957)
RT REV. DR. CASIMIR F. DURAND (1879-1957)
Deuxième évêque catholique-chrétien (vieux-catholique) francophone en Amérique
Second French-Speaking Christian Catholic (Old Catholic) Bishop in America

Dossier No C-31A
File No. C-31A

Fonds des Archives Nationales du Québec (ANQ) sur les vieux-catholiques francophones d'Amérique (Rite catholique-chrétien de la Section canadienne du CIÉC) - Collection No JB1983
Fund of the French-speaking Old Catholics in America at the National Archives of Quebec (NAQ) (Christian Catholic Rite of the Canadian Section of the ICCC) - Collection No. JB1983

DÉCLARATION - DECLARATION

Nous, soussignés, Messieurs Paul et René Durand, fils jumeaux de Mgr Casimir F. Durand, âgés de 80 ans et vivant au Minnesota, États-Unis, ainsi que Mgr Serge A. Thériault, 4e évêque ordinaire du Rite catholique-chrétien et responsable du Conseil international des Églises communautaires au Canada, déclarons ce qui suit:

Nous ajoutons à la Collection JB1983 des ANQ le Dossier C-31A sur Mgr Casimir F. Durand, accompagnié de la notice biographique suivante, établie au meilleur de nos connaissances:

* Né à La Révolte (Drôme), France, 1879.09.19, fils de Jean-Antoine Durand et de Julie Chancel.
* Venu au Canada comme missionnaire au début du siècle (St-Boniface, Manitoba).
* Joignit le rite catholique-chrétien sous Mgr Vilatte vers 1910 et exerça le saint ministère à Minneapolis, Minnesota. Fut également chapelain de Mgr Vilatte et chancelier diocésain.
* Devint le 2e évêque catholique-chrétien de langue française en Amérique en 1926. Fut consacré le 16 septembre (+Axel Z. Fryxell).
* Épousa Anna Mansipe et eût avec elle deux garçons jumeaux, Paul et René, élevés à Prior Lake, Minnesota, à partir de 1932.
* Exerça la médecine à Minneapolis.
* Est décédé à Prior Lake, Minnesota, le 6 janvier 1957. Inhumé à Pior Lake.

Le Dossier C-31A comprendra des souvenirs, des lettres et des découpures de journaux, ainsi qu'une photo fournis par MM. Paul et René Durand.

We, the undersigned, Paul and René Durand, twin sons of Bishop Casimir F. Durand, 80 years old and residing in the State of Minnesota, U.S.A., and the Most Rev. Serge A. Theriault, 4th Bishop Ordinary, Christian Catholic Rite, and General Superintendent for Canada, International Council of Community Churches, do declare the following:

We add to Collection No. JB1983 of QNA File C-31A, on the Rt Rev. Dr. Casimir F. Durand, accompanied with this biographical notice, which is accurate to the best of our knowledge:

* Born in La Révolte (Drôme), France, on September 19, 1879, the son of Jean-Antoine Durand and Julie Chancel.
* Came to Canada as a missionary at the turn of the century. Worked in Manitoba.
* Joined the Christian Catholic (Old Catholic) Movement under Bishop J.R. Vilatte. Became parish priest in Minneapolis, Minnesota. Was also Bp Vilatte's chaplain and diocesan chancellor.
* Became second French-speaking Christian Catholic (Old Catholic) Bishop in America and was consecrated 1926.09.16 (+Axel Z. Fryxell).
* Married Anna Mansipe and had with her two twin sons: Paul and René, brought up in Prior Lake, Minnesota.
* Practiced medicine in Minneapolis.
* Died in Prior Lake, Minnesota, on January 6, 1957, where he has been buried.

File No. C-31A will contain memorabilia, letters, clippings and a photograph supplied by Mr. Paul and René Durand from Minnesota.

Paul C. Durand
Paul Durand

René E. Durand
René Durand

April 20, 1997
Date

+ Serge A. Thériault
+ Serge A. Thériault

Diane Chouinard
Witness - Témoin

1997.04.15
Date

12
Biographical Sketches: Paul and Rene Durand

Paul Durand
Oct. 24, 1917 – June 2, 2007

Named Paul after Bishop Paolo Miraglia-Gullotti, his godfather.

Honorary member of the Society of the Precious Blood.

Husband of Dorothy (Anderson) and father of Brian (Robin) & Susan (Dean) Busse.

Spent four years in the Army during World War II.

Was employed by the federal government, working in administration at the VA Hospital in Minneapolis and also at Fort Snelling.

Rene Durand
Oct. 24, 1917 – Sept. 28, 2005

Named Rene after Bishop Rene Vilatte, his godfather.

Honorary member of the Society of the Precious Blood.

Husband of Helen (Lundberg) and father of Annette (Fedler) and Bonnie (Norman).

Was a sgt in US Army during World War II.

Worked as a commercial artist, designing rings during the day, painting in his off time and showing at different shows. "We are blessed with many of

He was a humble man who found real joy in the simple pleasures of life. His lifelong passion was researching Dakota Indian place names and legends. Paul had published books on this subject.[108]

He is buried in Maple Lawn Cemetery, Faribault, Minnesota.

his paintings, wrote his daughter Bonnie. His artistic talent mostly came from his mother – we have her paintings. He loved the outdoors, canoeing, and no one told stories like he could."

He is buried in Rice Lake Cemetery, Dodge County, Minnesota.

[108] Durand, Paul C. Ta-ku-wa-kan ti-pi: Dwelling place of the gods: the Dakota homeland in the Twin Cities metropolitan area. Prior Lake, MN: The author, 1982. Durand, Paul C. Where the waters gather and the rivers meet: an atlas of the eastern Sioux. Prior Lake, MN: P.C. Durand, 1994.

INDEX

A

Abbey of St. Anthony: 10, 64

Acts of: charity, contrition, faith & hope: 110

Africa: 37, 94

African Americans: 13, 20, 121

African Orthodox Church (A.O.C.): 13, 35

Alberic: 77

Alexander, Daniel: 37

Algonquian: 10

American Catholic Church (A.C.C.): 7, 8, 20, 31, 35, 79-83, 104, 120-123, 126, 127, 129
- African American constituency: see African Orthodox Church
- Consistory of: 120
- Council of churches: 7, 21
- Extension in France: 14, 36
- French-speaking constituency: see Christian Catholic Church
- German American constituency: 121
- Incorporation of: 21
  - Amendment to Articles of: 130
- Polish constituency: 18, 121
- Protocol: 93
- Swedish American constituency: see Swedish Church in America
- Synod: 18, 31, 32
- Theological Department of: 13

America: 80, 94, 119

American School of Naturopathy: 10

Americanism: 80

Anacletus: 120

Anderson, Charles P.: 79

Anglican(s) / Anglicanism : 68, 80, 119

Anima Christi: 117

Antioch / See of the East: 7, 19, 26, 93, 104, 119, 127

Antonines (Antonians): 64

Apostles Creed: 106-109

Apostolic succession: 7, 19, 26, 31, 93, 104, 120, 127, 129

Arabs: 63

Archbishop of Utrecht (Old Catholic): 19

Archives Nationales du Québec (C.C.C. Holding): 20, 131

Asia Minor : 80

Assiniboin: 10

Augustinian rule: 9

Austro-Hungarian: 19

B

Barbarian(s): 76, 77

Baronius, Caesar: 120

Basel: see Council(s)

Beatitudes (8): 115

Beckwith, Edwin B: 12, 28

Belgium: 71, 74

Bellarmine, Robert: 123

Benoît, Paul: 10

Beranger of Friuli: 77

Bernard of Clairvaux: see St. Bernard of Clairvaux

Bodot, J. Nicholas: 16, 38, 121

Bologna (Italy): 77

Border Cities Hospital: 13

Boryszewski, Francis I.: 18, 121

Bossuet, Jacques Bénigne: 68, 71, 126

Bourassa, Henri: 17

Bricaud, Jean: 14

Brotherhood of St. Anthony : see Monks of St. Anthony

Buddist: 99

Buffalo NY: 93, 95

Byzantine Empire: 78

C

Caesarius : see St. Caesarius of Arles

California: 8

Canada: 8, 9, 18, 19, 21, 127, 131

Canons Regular of the Immaculate Conception (C.R.I.C.): 8-10, 64

Canons Regular of St Augustine: 83

Canterbury: 26, 81

Capua (Italy): 123

Catechism: 8, 12, 103

Catholic, Catholicity, Catholicism: 80-82, 97, 99, 104, 123

Catholic test: 58

Chancel, Julie: 9, 131

Charlemagne: 76

Chicago IL: 7, 8, 11, 18, 20, 21, 26, 79

Chicago Tribune: 12, 79

Chiniquy, Charles: 7

Chouinard, Diane: 131

Christ:
- Master of his Church: 50
- Only Mediator & Savior: 48, 101

Commandments of the Church: 113

Confiteor: 110

Constance: see Council(s)

Constantine I: 76, 78

Constantine XI: 78

Constantinople: 75, 78

Côté, O'Neill: 19, 42

Council(s) :
- Above the pope : 68
- Bethleem : 100
- Constance & Basel : 68
- Ecumenical : 46, 54, 58, 59, 94, 97, 100
- General : 54, 99, 129
- Nicea : 123
- Trent : 100
- Troyes : 69
- Vatican (1870) : 46, 71, 124

Cree: 10

Croatia: 124

Croisades: 63

Cross of Lorraine: 90

Crown of Thorns of Jesus Christ: 14

Cultuelles (Associations): 125

Czernohorsky-Fehervary, Tomaz: 19, 41

D

Dakota (Indians): 10, 134

Dauphiné (France): 64

Desantis: 120

Des Houx, Henri: 125

De Unanumo, Miguel: 126

DiFlorio, Patricia D.: 16

Dionysius: see St Dionysius of Paris

Doctrinal statement: see Profession of faith

Doctrine: 48-51, 68, 100, 129
- Of Intention: 120

Dogmas: 48-53, 58, 71, 100, 126, 129

Donation of Constantine: 76, 123

Dosithos Nataras: 100

Drolet, Michel: 7

D'Hulst, Maurice Le Sage d'Hauteroche : 125

Dupanloup, Felix, Antoine, Philibert : 71

Durand, J. Antoine: 9, 131

Durand, Paul: 8, 12-14, 21, 40, 131, 133

Durand, Rene: 8, 12, 14, 40, 131, 133

Duval (Kewaunee) WI: 124

French Academie: 71

French-speaking constituency: see Christian Catholic Church

Franco-American(s): 16, 17, 123
- Churches: 16, 17
- Parish (A.C.C.): see Christian Catholic Church

Franz Ferdinand of Austria: 74

Fryxell, Axell Z.: 15, 18, 21, 38, 121, 131

G

Gallican, Gallicanism: 11, 17, 68, 71, 74, 75, 126

Garvey, Markus: 13

Gatineau (Quebec): 7

Gaul(s) : 68, 71

Genevieve : see St Genevieve of Paris

Germany: 10

Giles Hermit : 72

Glandage (Drôme, France): 9, 23

Gondards Cemetery (Versailles, France): 18

Good Shepherd Cathedral Chapel (A.O.C.): 14

Goodrich, Peter W.: 19, 42

Grace before meal: 118

Grea, Adrien: 64

Great Britain: 18

Great Schism: 76

Greek Orthodox Church: 100

Greeks: 77

Gregory II: 123

Gregory VII: 78

Gul Gerard: 19

Guette, Wladimir: 47

H

Harispe, Pierre: 125

Henry IV: 78

Herbal medicine, herbalism, herbalist: 10, 11, 65

Hickey, William: 16, 123

Hildebrand of Sovana: see Gregory VII

Hilary: see St Hilary of Poitiers

Hindu: 99

Hinton, Daniel C.: 7, 18, 20, 21, 129

Holy Land: 14

Holy Orders: 83

Holy Spirit:
- Seven gifts of: 113
- Twelve fruits of: 114

Homberger , William Oscar: 21, 121

Homeopathic Medical School, University of Michigan: 11

Homer, William Oscar: see Homberger

Honorat: see St Honorat of Arles

Hospital (Hospitaller) Brothers of St Anthony: see Monks of St Anthony

Hugues: see St Hughes of Grenoble

Hungarian:
• Revolt: 19

Hungary: 19, 71

I

Illinois: 7, 21, 26, 32, 119

Imperium: 53

Independent Catholic Church
• of Canada: 19
• of Sri Lanka: 7

Infallibility: see Papal infallibility and Church infallibility

Ignatius Peter III : 127

Institut Catholique de Paris: 125

International Council of Community Churches: 7, 130

Irenaeus: see St Irenaeus of Lyon

Italian Americans: 7, 12, 121

Italy: 71, 77, 80

J

James Bay (Canada): 10

Jesuits: 123

Jefferson Medical College: 13

Jew(s): 99

John X: 77

Jouanny, A.: 18

Journal de Rome: 125

Justification: 100

K

Kaminski, Stephen: 93

Kankakee IL: 7

Kanski, Francis: 18, 21, 27, 121

Kanyiles, Daniel: 37

Kneipp, Sebastian: 10, 11, 30

Knights Templar: 69

Kowalski, Jan Michal: 19

Kozlowska, Feliksa: 19

L

Lando (Landus) : 77

Langelier, Moise: 7

Labeaume (France): 11

La Nouvelle Revue : 125

Last things : 116

La Sentinelle (newspaper) : 17, 123

Lamenais, Hugues Félicité Robert de : 125

Latin Rite : 94

Lavaute (Sicard de), family: 16

Law on Religious Corporations of Quebec: 21

Law on the Separation of the Churches and the State (France): 125

Le Devoir (newspaper) : 17

Liberalism: 58

Lindlahr College of Natural Therapeutics: 11, 30

Lindlahr, Henry: 11, 30, 87, 90

Lindlahr Sanitorium: 13, 87, 90, 91

Lines, Gregory: 18

Liturgy: 60

Lloyd, Frederick E.J.: 7, 8, 12, 18-21, 26, 27, 31, 38, 103, 119, 121

Los Angeles CA: 18

Lust, Benedict: 10

Lutheranism: 80

Lyon (France): 14

M

MacMillan, Michael C.: 18

Mancip, Anna de (Mrs C.F. Durand): 11, 12, 14, 21, 38, 40, 131

Manitoba (Canada): 9, 10, 13

Mansipe: see Mancip

Mariavite(s): 18-19

Marozia: 77

Martin of Tours: see St Martin of Tours

Mary, mother of the Lord: see St. Mary

Materialism, Materialist(s): 76, 94

Miami FL: 18

Muehler, J.N. & Marianne family : 16

N

Native ministry : 10

National Assembly (Parliament) of Quebec: 16

National Council of the Churches of Christ in the U.S.A.: 13

Nationalism: 18

Natural health practice: 10, 63

Nature Cure: 11, 87, 90, 91

Naturopathic College : 10

Naturopathic Medicine (Naturopathy), Naturopathic Doctor : 8, 10-12

Neth, Joseph Edward: 42

New York: 10

Niagara Falls (Canada): 19, 42

Nicolas I: 45

Nincheri, Guido: 16

Norman, Bonnie (Durand): 8, 133, 134

North America : 10

Norwood Park (Chicago): 35

Notable duties: 116

P

Pont Colbert (Common Observance) Cistercian Abbey : 14

Prayer for the dead: 111

Presbyterianism: 80

Prior Lake MN : 21, 40, 131

Priscitelli, Vincent E. : 121

Pro-Cathedral Church of All Saints, Seattle: 38

Prochniewski, Roman J. : 18, 19, 41

Protestant, Protestantism: 82, 100, 104

Profession of faith : 7, 31, 32

Providence RI : 16

Q

Quebec
- City: 10
- Province (Canada): 7, 19

R

Rationalist(s): 94

Ravenna: 77

Reform:
- Ecclesial: 53-56
- Results of: 58-60
- Theological: 48-52

Remi: see St Remi of Reims

Repentance: 116

Revue de métaphysique et de morale : 126

Rhône-Alpes (France): 9

Robertson, W. Ernest: 13, 14, 35-37

Robillard, Anselme: 7

Roman Catholic
- Bishops: 120
- Claims: 76
- Curia: 11, 75, 78, 126
- Falsifications: 47
- Innovations: 46
- Orders: 19, 120

Roman empire: 67, 75, 76, 100, 124

Rome: 81, 119, 123
- Bishop, Bishopric (see) of: 75, 76, 120, 124
- Christian center: 78
- Church of: 120
- City: 76
- Western Patriarchate: 94

Rumilly, Robert: 17

S

Sacramental grace: 120

Sacraments: 100

Sacred Hearth Polish National Church: 15, 38

Sacrosancta (decree): 68

Saint Antoine l'Abbaye (Isère, France) : 9, 11, 23

Saint Claude (Jura), Switzerland: 9

Saint Paul MN: 10, 15

Saint Ursula Falls (Quebec, Canada): 16

Santiago de Compostella: 71

Saracens: 63

Saskatchewan (Canada): 10

Scheel, John H.: 10

Scotland: 80

Scripture/Bible: 48, 52, 55, 99, 100, 121

Seattle WA : 18, 38

Serbia: 74

Shrine of St Anthony: see Abbey of St Anthony

Sibley, Churchill : 18

Sign of the Cross: 105

Sins:
- Against the Holy Spirit: 116
- Mortal: 115
- Ways of sharing in: 115

Siple, William: 21, 130

St Hilary of Poitiers: 72

St Honorat of Arles: 72

St Hugues of Grenoble: 72

St Irenaeus of Lyon: 72

St Isidore of Seville: 123

St Joseph Oratory, Montreal: 16

St Louis, King of France: 14, 72, 73

St Martin of Tours: 71

St Mary: 19, 100, 129

St Paul Apostle: 124

St Peter Apostle: 19, 26, 55, 75, 77, 93, 104, 119, 124, 127

St Remi of Reims: 72

St Vincent of Lerins: 49, 72, 125

Strossmayer, Josip: 124

Sullivan, W.: 20, 83

Swedish Church in America (A.C.C.): 15, 38, 121

Syllabus Errorum: 58

Sylvester I: 123

Synod: 54, 55, 59
- Of Jerusalem: see Council of Bethleem

Syracuse NY: 16

Syriac Orthodox Patriarchate: 7, 127

T

U

Ultramontanes, Ultramontanism : 18, 67, 68, 75

Union of Christian Churches : 47, 56, 57

Union Saint Jean Baptiste d'Amérique : 17

U.S.A. : 10, 11, 13, 26, 79, 81, 104, 121, 127

V

Valla, Lorenzo : 76

Versailles (France) : 14, 18

Vincent of Lerins : see St Vincent of Lerins

Vilatte, René : 7, 8, 11, 12, 14, 16, 18, 20, 21, 26, 27, 31-36, 67, 93, 104, 124, 125, 131, 133

Virtues :
- Cardinal : 113
- Contrary to mortal sins : 115
- Theologal : 113

W

Warsaw (Poland) : 19, 38

West Indies : 13

Windsor (Ontario, Canada) : 8, 13, 30

Wisconsin : 7, 21

Woonsocket RI : 16, 17, 123

Words of Christ on the Cross (7): 116

Works of mercy :
- Seven corporal : 114
- Seven spiritual : 114

World War I : 74

World War II : 133

X, Y, Z

Yugosavia, Yugoslav : 74

BIBLE PASSAGES USED BY BISHOP DURAND

Ephesians 4:3	Unity depends more upon the exercise of the members' moral qualities than the structure of the institution.
	Endeavouring to keep the unity of the Spirit in the bond of peace.
Ephesians 4:4-6	The doctrine of unity: reason for pursuing peace.
	There is one body and one Spirit, just as also you were called in one hope of your calling; one Lord, one faith, one baptism, one God and Father of all who is over all and through all and in all.
Galatians 2:20	To become one with Christ, a person must be willing not only to give up sin, but also to surrender his whole way of looking at things.
	I have been crucified with Christ and I no longer live, but Christ lives in me. The life I now live in the body, I live by faith in the Son of God, who loved me and gave himself for me.
John 17:22	When people come together, across the boundaries that divide humans, they realize that our perfection, our unity, our becoming one, is found in Christ.
	I have given them the glory that you gave me, that they may be one as we are one.

Jude 1: 3   We need to contend for the faith as there are those who deny the authority of God and Jesus.

I urge you to contend for the faith that was once for all delivered to the saints.

Matthew 16:18   The rock on which Christ builds his church is Peter's confession of faith: You are Christ, the Son of the Living God.

Thou art Peter and upon this rock I will build my Church.

Matthew 18:17   The infallible, heavenly authority of the Church is the community of the believers filled and led by the Holy Spirit.

Take your case to the Church.

Matthew 18:20   Bringing brothers and sisters back into harmony with one another. Jesus is saying, when this type of reconciliation takes place it is the type of thing He wants to be a part of.

Where two or three are gathered together in my name, there am I in the midst of them.

Matthew 23:8   Limiting any danger there may be of a believer becoming more important than the people he's called to serve.

Be not called Rabbi: for one is your Master, Jesus Christ.

Matthew 28:19

Teaching is required to make disciples. Preaching the gospel to the world begins the process of teaching. Disciples are created through steady feeding, a believing response in those who hear the Word of God.

Go ye therefore, and teach all nations.

1 Peter 5:2

Pastors should not rule their flock with force, nor hold the office because of what they can get out of it.

Oversee the flock of God not constrainedly, according to His will; not for sordid gain.

1 Thessalonians 5:21

Instead of laying aside reason in matters of revelation, we have the right to test it by Scripture.

Prove all things; hold fast that which is good.

ILLUSTRATIONS

List of Illustrations

The illustrations used in this book are all in the public domain (copyright expired or released) or belong to the C.C.C., except those indicated otherwise.

30: Homeopathic Medical School, University of Michigan.

Lindlahr College, Chicago.

Dr. Henry Lindlahr, M.D., 1862-1924.

Father Sebastian Kneipp, 1821-1897.

Registration Card: C.F. Durand, Missionary Priest at Windsor, Ontario, Canada.

31 : Letter of Bishop Vilatte to Bishop Lloyd, 1920.03.17.

34: Primatial Seal of Bishop Vilatte.

35: Consecration certificate of Bishop George A. McGuire bearing the signature of Bishop (then Fr.) Durand, 1921.

36: Carte de Visite of Bishop Vilatte and his Bull allowing the consecration of Rev. W. Ernest Robertson, 1923.

37: Bishops McGuire and Robertson at the consecration of Msgr. Daniel Alexander of South Africa, with Bishop Arthur S. Trotman, 1927.

38: Bishop Axel Z. Fryxell, 1860-1934.

Bishop Durand's mozetta.

Rev. Dr. J. Nicholas Bodot, D.C.

Rev. Kazimierz Krysinski, Rector of Sacred Heart Polish Church, Minneapolis.

39:     Cover of the book *Fiat Lux*.

Henri Perdriau, 1877-1950.

Bishop Durand's Imprimatur.

Nicollet Avenue, Minneapolis, where Bishop Durand's church was located, 1930s.

40:     Bishop Durand and his sons Paul & Rene, 1941.

Bishop Durand with his wife Anna in their garden at Prior Lake, Minnesota, 1950s.

41:     Archbishop Roman James Prochniewski and Bishop Fehervary in Plock Cathedral, 1945.

Msgr. Côté mitred by Msgr. Fehervary, 1974.

Msgr. Côté with Archbishops Peter W. Goodrich and Joseph Edward Neth in Niagara Falls, 1978.

48:     Icon of Christ the Teacher.
        http://marianland.com

49:     Icon of St. Vincent of Lerins.
        archangelsbooks.com

51 :   Painting: the Teaching Church.

54 :   The Synod of Dordrecht. Gravue by Bernard Picart, 1673-1733.
        http://da.wikipedia.org/wiki/Fil:Synodedordrecht.jpg

BIBLIOGRAPHY

1

Works of Bishop Durand

ESSAYS

National Churches Dominated by the Roman Curia and Being Suppressed, Chicago, 1916.

Taking Care of the Body as Well as the Soul with the Natural Healing Methods Learnt from the Old Monks of St. Anthony, Minneapolis, 1932.

The Call of the American Catholic Church, Chicago, 1917.

The Old Catholic Church, Woonsocket RI, 1928.

LETTERS

I congratulate and admire you. To Bishop Rene Vilatte, 1914.

I accept the Presidency of the A.C.C. To Reverend W. Sullivan, July 15, 1940.

POEM

Free, Catholic and Gallican, 1915.

2

Books, Articles, Testimonials About Bishop Durand or Having Relation to Him and His Work

Dr. C.F. Durand Consecrated an Old Catholic Bishop, Twin Cities newspaper, Minneapolis/Saint Paul, September 15, 1926.

Henri Bourassa, *Schisme gallican orthodoxe*, Le Devoir, Montreal, January 17, 1928.

Armand Chartier, Histoire des Franco-Américains de la Nouvelle-Angleterre, 1775-1900, Septentrion ed., 1991.

Robert Chodos & Eric Hamovitch, Quebec and the American Dream, Between the Lines, 1991, p. 116.

Le Travailleur, weekly paper, Worcester MA, October 15, 1959.

J. Albert Foisy, The Sentinellist Agitation in New England, 1925-1928, Providence Visitor Press, 1930, Chapter 18.

L'Intermédiaire des chercheurs et curieux: Volume 25, 1975.

New Incorporations, The Monetary Times, Toronto, August 11, 1922, p. 10.

Yves Roby, The Franco-Americans of New England: Dreams and Realities, Septentrion ed., 2004, page 262.

Robert Rumilly, Henri Bourassa : la vie publique d'un grand Canadien, Chanteclerc ed., 1953, p. 708 & 710.

Robert Rumilly, Histoire des Franco-Américains, Union Saint-Jean-Baptiste d'Amérique, 1958, p. 432 & 445.

University of Michigan, Homoeopathic Medical School, Annual Announcement: Graduates, Ann Arbor, 1913, p. 108

3

Rev. C.F. Durand in the <u>Chicago Tribune</u>: Sermons & Services in Chicago Churches

1916.02.05: St. David's Mission, 33 E. 3rd St. Mass, 8:00 A.M.

1917.05.05: St. David's House & Chapel. 2050 Prairie Ave. C.F. Durand. Divine Iiturgy 10:30 A.M. Bishop Lloyd will preach.

1917.05.20: "The Call of the American Catholic Church," the Rev. C. F. Durand.

1917.05.26: American Catholic Church, 2350 Prairie Ave. Rev. C. F. Durand. Holy Mass. 10:30 A.M. Mass daily. 7:30 A. M.

1917.06.03: C.F. Durand and the Rev. Timothy Peshkoff. Bishop Lloyd preached the sermon. A congratulatory address and gift were presented to Archbishop Vilatte, Primate of the American Catholic Church following the service.

1917.06.09: Holy Mass and Ordination of Deacon E.J. Higgins to the Priesthood, 10:30 A.M.

1917.06.16: American Catholic Church, 2050 Prairie Ave. C.F. Dueand, Priest in charge. Rev. Father Higgins will say his First Mass at 10:30 A.M. Bishop Lloyd will preach.

1917.07.14: American Catholic Church, 2050 Prairie Ave. Rt Rev. F.E.J. Lloyd. D.D., Bishop of Illinois. C.F. Durand Priest in charge. Rev. E.J. Higgins, Assistant Priest. Mass. 8 and 11 a.m. Bishop Lloyd will preach at the 11:00 Mass.

1917.09.01: American Catholic Church, 2050 Prairie Ave. Holy Mass at 8:00 and 11:00 A.M. Rt. Rev. Bishop Lloyd will preach at the 11:00 A.M. Mass: "Peace and the Bishop of Rome."

4

Books and Articles About the A.C.C. and the C.C.C., or Having Relation to them

Daniel C. Hinton, *Statement about the A.C.C.*, The Crusader, Chicago, November 1936.

Frederick E.J. Lloyd, The Smaller Catechism for the Use of American Catholics, Chicago, 1915.

Paolo Miraglia-Gullotti, *Fredericus Lloyd Americae Episcopus*, Chicago, 1915.

Paolo Miraglia-Gullotti, Why the American Catholic Church Cannot Accept Roman Catholic Orders, Chicago, 1917.

Serge A. Theriault, Msgr. Rene Vilatte, Community Organizer of Religion, Apocryphile Press, Berkeley, 2006.

The American Catholic Church Starts Its Session on Sunday, Chicago Tribune, September 27, 1929.

Rene Vilatte, What was Catholic once must be forever, Chicago, 1914.

Rene Vilatte, We maintain the faith once for all given to the Saints, Chicago, 1910.

The Negro Churchman, Vol. 8, No. 6, June-July 1930.

Theriault, Serge A., *Charles Chiniquy et les églises catholiques-chrétiennes*, Aujourd'hui Credo, United Church of Canada, November 1999.

The Year Book of the Churches 1924, Federal Council of the Churches of Christ in America, New York, p. 13.

Year Book of the Churches, National Council of the Churches of Christ in the U.S.A., New York, 1919, p. 78.

5

Books on Gallicanism, Old Catholicism and Ultramontanism

Miguel de Unanumo, *La foi pascalienne*, Revue de Métaphysique et de Morale, no 2 (1923), pp. 345-349.

Wladimir Guettee, La Papauté hérétique, Sandoz & Fishbacher ed., Paris, 1874.

Michael C. MacMillan, *The Character of Henri Bourassa's Political Philosophy*, American Review of Canadian Studies 1982b 12(1): 10-29.

Eugene Michaud, La Papauté antichrétienne, Sandoz & Fishbacher, 1873.

Henri Perdriau, Fiat Lux : Le bon sens et la logique, La Vérité Publisher, Woonsocket RI, 1928.

Serge A. Theriault, Msgr. Dominique M. Varlet, Originator of the Old Catholic Episcopal Succession, 1678-1742, Apocryphile Press, Berkeley CA, 2010.

6

Other publications of interest

Patricia D. DiFlorio, <u>John Nicholas and Marianne Muehler Bodot Family</u>, Syracuse NY, 2007, p. 7

Durand, Paul C. <u>Ta-ku-wa-kan ti-pi: Dwelling place of the gods: the Dakota homeland in the Twin Cities metropolitan area,</u> Prior Lake, MN: The author, 1982.

Durand, Paul C. <u>Where the waters gather and the rivers meet: an atlas of the eastern Sioux</u> Prior Lake, MN: P.C. Durand, 1994.

7

Archives

Bibliothèque et Archives Nationales du Québec

C.C.C. Holding (Collection Réforme Catholique): P 103

- Series French-speaking Old Catholic Movement in America (S4)

- Series Msgr. Casimir F. Durand (S6) containing books, magazines, clippings and personal effects: episcopal garments, 4 candles, crucifix and altar prayer card from the parish in Minneapolis...

Notes